THE PATH OF PERFECTION
and REALM OF AFFLICTIONS

in
The METAPHYSICAL
and PHYSICAL REALMS

KIEN T. MAI, MD

Kien T Mai, MD, FRCPC,
Former Professor of Pathology, University of Ottawa,
General Practitioner for over 30 years
Meditation Practitioner for over 30 years
Author of more than 150 medical research articles and
more than 100 national and international presentations

**Author of the book: MEDITATION and THE SOUL in
NEUROSCIENCE:** *AN OVERVIEW
and ONTOLOGICAL VIEW.*
(Amazon Publishing Agency, April 2024)

*To many people, this book is similar to a cock crowing
at noon, rare and out of harmony of life,
But for you, hopefully, it will point out that
Life is not too short to enjoy
But a repetition of momentary episodes of pleasure
Serving the purpose of a springboard to overcome suffering
And finally reaching the Heavenly Morality and Perfection*
KM

*In a rubbish pit, there flourishes the lotus bloom fragrant
So among rubbish-beings, common humans blind-become,
the Perfect Buddha's pupil outshines with wisdom bright.*
Dhammapada

TABLE OF CONTENTS

PREFACE viii

Chapter I: CONCEPTS ABOUT HAPPINESS AND DEPRESSION x
I. PLEASURE AND PAIN: THE LAW OF THE WORLD OF DUALITY 5
II. THE SCIENCE OF PLEASURE-HAPPINESS AND PAIN- 6
A. SCIENCE OF PAIN AND PLEASURE 6
B. HAPPINESS AND DEPRESSION/MELANCHOLY 7
III. SCIENCE 9
SECOND THERMODYNAMIC LAW
IV. THE TAO OF HAPPINESS AND DEPRESSION 11
A. WHAT IS THE TAO? 11
PHILOSOPHY OF HAPPINESS AND SUFFERING 13
B. FAR EASTERN PHILOSOPHY 14
1. I CHING or Book of Change 14
2. Far Eastern philosophers. 15
C. WESTERN PHILOSOPHERS. 23
1. Happiness is pleasure minus suffering. 16
2. Hedonism: Hedonism seeks joy and avoids suffering 16
3. The hedonistic Utilitarianism 16
4. Psychological/motivational complacency 17
5. Pleasure is based on personal 17
6. Aesthetic pleasure 17
7. The school of Cyrene, ... 18
8. Democritus is considered the 'laughing philosopher' 18
9. Aristotle 384-322TTC uses the term eudaimonia to 18
10. Cynicism goes further than suffering and denies Happiness 18
11. Epicurus, Pyrrho, ... 18
12. Augustine of Hippo (354–430) 18
13. In resurrection time, ... 19
14. Philosophers from the Middle 19
15. Early modern period, ... 19
16. Currently Władysław Tatarkiêwicz (1886–1980) 19
Herbert Viktor Frankl 19
Robert Nozick 20
Michel Onfray 20
Jean Paul Sartre. 20
C. HAPPINESS AND SUFFERINGS IN RELIGIONS 20
1. CHRISTIANITY 21
Jean-Paul Sartre 24
2. BUDDHISM 24
a) Ten mental models 27
b) Seven Foolishness and Eight Inversions 27
c) The Four Noble Truths 28
Abdidhamma
121 Mind/Consciousness/Citta

Chapter II: 34

THE CREATION OF UNIVERSE WITH SUFFERING 34
I. THE CREATION OF UNIVERSE AND THE EMOTION. 37
A) According to Big Bang Theory (H1.2) 37
1. Big Bang 37
2. BARYONIC MATTER (MATTER SENSITIVE TO THE SENSES) IN THE PW AND PHYSICAL FORCES 39
3. NEUTRINO 40
B. THE CREATION OF THE INVISIBLE MATTER (NON-BARYONIC MATTER) 41
C. THE SOUL: AN INTERMEDIATE ENTITY BETWEEN THE METAPHYSICAL AND PHYSICAL REALMS. 42
1. IS THE SOUL A REALITY OR NOT? 42
2. COMPONENTS OF THE SOUL 44
3. The experiment of Dr Duncan McDougall and the Book of "The weigher of Souls 45
C. Further reading: PROPOSED HYPOTHESIS OF THE SOUL ARCHITECTURE. 45
II. THE EMPTINESS / VOID, VACUUM 48
A. In PHYSICS. 48
B. In the brain. 48
D. CHRISTIANITY 48
H. SPINOZA AND METAPHISICAL CONCEPT, ... 48
III. THE EMPTINESS / VOID, VACUUM. 50
A. EASTERN PHILOSOPHY: THECONCEPT 50
B. HINDUISM /Kena Upanishads 53
C. BUDDHISM 53
IV. EMPTINESS POSTULATE, EMPTINESS AS A POSTULATE, ORIGIN OF UNIVERSE. EMPTINESS IS MIRACULOUSLY EXISTENCE 54
A. EMPTINESS IS BUDDHAHOOD 54
Buddhist Sutra. 54
B. CONTROVERSIAL INTERPRETATIONS OF BUDDHA'S TEACHINGS REGARDING THE EMPTINESS. 56
C, THE WORLD, AS A FALSE PERCEPTION/ PROJECTION) 58
D. WHY, IN CHRISTIANITY OR BUDDHISM, IS THERE NO MENTION OF THE TREMENDOUS ENERGY AND TEMPERATURE RELEASED AT THE CREATION? 59
E. FALSE THOUGHT FROM THE EMPTINESS VERSUS BIG BANG SINGULARITY. 60
F. CHARACTERISTICS OF EM 60
a) Three self natures, noumental characteristics, Prakriti or 61
b) Eight negativities: 61
c) Other aributes are: 61
6. Morphic Field
G. PARAMITA and SELFLESSNESS 65
V. UNDERSTANDING OF THE IGNORANCE and THREE SEALS OF DHARMA, Four Kinds of Mindfulness Eightfold Path 68
a) Buddha recommends the technique of Four Kinds of Mindfulness. 69
b) Ontological Method 69
VI. The Darwin Theory G. DARWINISM. 70
1. The theory. 70

v

2. Social Darwinism. 70
3. Origin of life. 71
4. The Cell Theory. 71
5. Gap in the evolution. 72
6. The first Man and Woman (suggestive of Adam and Eva in the Paradise in The Old Testament are doubtful) ?**72**
   VII. THE CREATION OF SPECIES. 78
   VIII. HOW DOES THE CREATION HAPPEN? BY CHANCE OR BY 82
   Role of the Ultimate Omniscience..82
IX. REASON OF CREATION. 83
   X. EMBODIED SOUL OF THE PHYSICAL PARTS WITHOUT BRAIN 86
   A.   EMBODIED SOUL 86
   B. Abdidhamma 86
C. The Emotion 86
XI. COMMUNICATION BETWEEN DIFFERENT MINDS/SOULS 87

Chapter III: UNIVERSE VERSUS MULTIVERSE. 88
Introduction..89
I. Einstein's Theory of Relativity and Bohr's Quantum Interpretation.....89
II. The Multiverse of Hugh Everett..89
III. The view of Sir Penrose. 90
IV. Findings in the Old Testament 91
V. Buddhism...92

Chapter IV: VEIL OF IGNORANCE. 94
Summary 94
Introduction. 95
I. AFTER THE CREATION. 95
II. Veil of Ignorance 96
   ROLE OF ATTENTION IN THE FORMATION OF CS98
A. Ananda,...96
B. Veil of Ignorance 97
C. CS limits the UO. 100
1 Role Of The Attention In The Generation Of CS 100
1. Parikalpita..101
2. Paratantra (Relative knowledge/ vn: Y tha Sở Tánh): 101
3. Parinishpanna 102
   KURT GODEL'S INCOMPLETENESS THEOREMS AND THE VEIL OF   99

Chapter V: THE METAPHYSICAL WORLD: SIENCE IN IN THE SUPRALUMINAL SPEED AND MIIRACLEs..108
Summary 108
Introduction 110
I. UO IN RELIGIONS. 111
   II. THE PHYSICAL AND METAPHYSICAL WORLDS. 113
   III. TRAVEL WITH SUPRALUMINAL SPEED 114
   IV. MIRACLES IN THE MW. 119
   V. The meaning of praying..122
   VI. The character of the MW...126

V. BUDDHA'S LIGHT OR INFINITE LIGHT EXPERIENCED IN THE MEDITATION. 126
VI. THE PURE LAND OF AMITABA BUDDHA and WESTERN WORLD OF ULTIMATE BLISS..126
VII. THE WORLD OF DUALITY: NIRVANA OR HIGH LEVEL OF HEAVEN..127
A. NIRVANA 128
B. HEAVEN. 131
NON- DUALIISTIC PATHWAY   125

Chapter VI:
THE PHYSICAL WORLD IS THE PATH OF PERFECTION BY RE-EDUCATION TO ATTAIN HAPPINESS AND ULTIMAT TRUTH.133
I. THE VISIBLE WORLD/PHYSICAL WORLD..135
II. WHY IS THERE THE VISIBLE/PHYSICAL WORLD.135
CHRISTANITY.135
.B. BUDDHISM
III. THE WORLD OF HUMANS AND ANIMALS. 142
.A. THE PHYSICAL WORLD 142
1. PHOTONS..142
2. The four fundamental forces in physics and Dark Force143
Grand Unified Theory GUT. 143
Theory of Everything TOE...144
3. THE SOUL. 144
IV. THE METAPHYSICAL WORLD IS THE SOUL'S HOME LAND. 144
V. THE PHYSICAL WORLD IS MADE FOR THE SINNERS....................145
Ascetism in Buddhism..153
Acetism in Christianity...155
VI. THE METAPHYSICAL WORLD IS THE MAIN PART OF THE CREATION.155
VII. THE MEANING OF THE LORD'S REDEMPTION OF MANKIND IN THE PHYSICAL WORLD 156
VIII. THE MEANING OF LAW AND THE REDEMPTION 159
THE TWELVE LINKS OF DEPENDENT ORIGINATION

CONCLUSIONS..159
WHO IS THE CREATOR/GOD?. 163
THE CREATION INITIATED BY FALSE THOUGHT 163
i. REALM OF GRAVITY AND DARK MATTER......................................164
ii. PHYSICAL WORLD/REALM..164

PREFACE.

Suffering mixed with joy belongs to the human world. Genuine and unmixed Goodness and Happiness belong to the Metaphysical Realm/World/MW. Different from the Physical Realm, the Metaphysical Realm is what humans can only feel but has never been proven by Science and Consciousness. The articles in this book, although of a metaphysical nature, are not imagination or illusion like in novels or movies. The articles are based on the Holy revelation in Christian Testaments and of Lord Buddha's teachings, which are recorded in Buddhist scriptures, with Jesus and Buddha's unerring words. Description of the phenomenon MW is built on theories that are both scientific and rational and based on established common events repeated from ancient times to the present day, such as the existence of the Soul, the light of Heaven or Buddha light, and other supernatural phenomena. Science always denies the fixed nature of continuously occurring biological phenomena because Science is limited to the Quantum threshold (although beyond-Quantum matter must exist, Science cannot know it; for example, Photons have zero weight because Photons are just the most subtle limit of the microscopic world of matter. Buddha said that when dividing visible matter billions and billions of billions of times, the end product becomes invisible and beyond Quantum particles) so it is called Emptiness/EM. Therefore, when we divide visible matter into invisible beyond Quantum particles, it is called EM. EM does not contain visible Quantum particles but contains beyond Quantum particles, which are also matter but cannot be detected by the sentients' five sensory organs and Consciousness also called the six bandits). From EM, due to the Big Bang or Thought, Creator/God is realized, the Universe/Multiverse is born. The resulting Creation is composed of the Metaphysical world, including Dark Force and Dark Matter which are so magical, grandiose, and subtle that they cannot be visible or heard by humans. EM/Creator also creates the Tangible/Visible/Physical World/PW, which is made of Photons and other Quantum particles. The PW world has a very coarse structure as compared to the MW.

Creator/God is only The Oneness of Reality, the unthinkable, unimaginable, formless being with Power, and Mind innumerable times more significant than human beings, impossible in viewing and hearing. The Creator is the summation of all known, unknown, and impossibly known laws. On the contrary, humans are illusional entities with limited ability of awareness and extensive stupidity but with heightened, sinful, and false egos.

The Creator created the Universe with this MW and humans, but why did He create so much suffering for creatures and humans? Religion says that God and Buddha save suffering, the original sin, but humans are still constantly in suffering. God/Creator/Jesus, Buddha is omnipotent, omniscient, and infinitely compassionate, but despite supplications and prayers, suffering never ends, so lasting Happiness is always a distant thing in this world. However, sometimes, when we fruitfully pray for God's help, it is because God Buddha wants everyone to know about the MW and Omniscience so that people can practice and learn and know that the metaphysical realm is the home to return to. God/Jesus or Buddha does not personally help anyone and does not intentionally show it off.

In this book, readers will find the ultimate cause of the constant suffering that God Buddha never removed from humans. Readers will find the reason why overcoming suffering is a lesson for everyone in this Earthly world. Improving the Morality of Four Immeasurable Minds of Virtue, Kindness, Love. Joy sharing and detachment), without binding to Greed, Anger, Ignorance, Arrogance, Dubtfullness, Derision, Ingratitude, and Selflessness/or Charity Altruism is the path of liberation to go to the Realm of Truth, Goodness, and Beauty. Although the path is arduous and challenging, it is the shortest path that God has installed as a teaching tool for sinful people to improve their morality before regaining the MW after removing the veil of ignorance. The veil of ignorance is the brain, the human body, and Karma, which the Soul carries after leaving the physical body. The coarse matter of the physical world obscures the MW, where there is more wonderful and miraculous matter. The MW includes the entire Universe with the light of Heaven/Nirvana, the only place where there is Truth, Goodness, Beauty, and Eternal Happiness. Amitabha Buddha's Pure Land is a world of bliss without suffering, but the sentient beings there can only enjoy Happiness depending on their merit, and it is very difficult to practice to gain more merit. The Universe, made of Photons and other Quantum particles, is full of suffering but is easy to practice and practice to gain merit quickly. Buddhist Dharma is equal and does not favor any methods or religions.
KM

Summary

This book is based on the Holy revelation in the Testaments, Buddha's teachings, and Jesus and Buddha's unerring words. Description of the phenomenon MW is built on theories that are both scientific and rational and based on established everyday events repeated from ancient times to the present day, such as the existence of the Soul, the light of Heaven or Buddha light, and other supernatural phenomena. Science always denies the Metaphysical nature of continuously occurring phenomena because Science is limited to the Quantum threshold. This is consistent with Godel's incompleteness theorem. Buddha said that when visible matter is divided billions of times, the end product becomes invisible and beyond quantum particles, called emptiness/EM. EM does not contain visible quantum particles but particles beyond quantum, which is also matter but cannot be detected by the sentients' five sensory organs and consciousness. Following to the Big Bang or Thought and from EM, *The Creator is realized in the realm of Primordial Duaiity (Heaven or Nirvana)*, and the Universe/Multiverse is born. The resulting Creation is composed of the Metaphysical world, including Dark Force and Dark Matter, which are so magical, grandiose, and subtle that humans cannot see or hear it. MW is characterized by permanence and non-discrimination. There is only wonderful and miraculous matter and Happiness. EM/Creator also creates the Tangible/Visible /Physical World/PW, which is made of Photons and other Quantum particles. The PW has a very coarse structure compared to the MW, which is subjective to entropy, a universal thermodynamic law characterized by the non-concessional increased disturbance, i.e., a mixture of pain and pleasure. The matter of the PW slows down the velocity and represents the karma. Creator/God has similar Form and Quality as a human being and is only The Oneness of Reality with Form, Power, and Mind innumerable times more significant than human beings, unthinkable, unimaginable, impossible in viewing and hearing. On the contrary, humans are illusional entities with limited ability of awareness and extensive stupidity but with heightened, sinful, and false egos.

Why did God create so much suffering for creatures and humans in this PW? Religion says that God and Buddha save suffering, the original sin, but humans are still constantly suffering. God/Creator/Jesus, Buddha is omnipotent, omniscient, and infinitely compassionate, but despite supplications and prayers, suffering never ends, so lasting Happiness is always a distant thing in this world.

In this book, readers will find the ultimate cause of the constant suffering God Buddha never removed from humans. Readers will discover why overcoming suffering is a lesson for everyone in this Earthly world. Improving the Morality of Four Immeasurable Minds of Virtue, kindness, Love. Joy sharing and detachment) and Selflessness/or Charity and Altruism is the path of liberation to go to the Realm of Truth, Goodness, and Beauty. Although the route is arduous and challenging, it is the shortest path that God has installed as a teaching tool for sinful people to improve their morality before regaining the MW after removing the veil of ignorance. The veil of ignorance is the brain, the human body, and Karma, which the Soul carries with it after leaving the physical body. The coarse matter of the physical world obscures the MW. The MW includes the entire Universe with the light of Heaven/Nirvana, the only place where Truth, Goodness, Beauty, and Eternal Happiness exist. Amitabha Buddha's Pure Land is a world of bliss without suffering, but the sentient beings there can only enjoy Happiness depending on their merit, and it is tough to practice to gain more merit. The Universe, made of Photons and other Quantum particles, is entirely suffering but is easy to practice to gain merit quickly. Buddhist Dharma is equal and does not favor any methods or religions.

Chapter I: CONCEPTS ABOUT HAPPINESS AND DEPRESSION

Summary

Pleasure or Suffering and Happiness or Depression are two opposing states of emotions in the Physical World/PW or Visible World /VW or the world of Duality. Pleasure or Sadness is the current state, while Happiness or Depression is a more permanent state that only occurs for a certain time duration after a significant event. Emotion is the part of Knowledge/Consciousness/CS that has external expression. Non-emotional or emotional Consciousness is represented in language and action or is not expressed externally and is only used as an inner Consciousness model for future information. Because lasting pleasure has no sufferance, it can only be found in the world of Oneness, such as Nirvana and the ultimate Heaven.

Science has helped us understand emotions, but it cannot explain why people suffer so much. Eastern philosophy, including the I Ching (book of Change), recognizes suffering as an obvious event in life, allowing people to avoid suffering and endure it passively rather than ultimately resolve it. In the West, philosophers from ancient to modern times have searched for eternal happiness but never found it.

Tao differs from science and philosophy in that science and philosophy are based on postulates or reflections. On the contrary, Tao is based on revelation thanks to the Omniscience of God. Postulates or thoughts always change with time and space, so Science and Philosophy are not absolutely and permanently reliable. Unfortunately, Tao's writing or Holy scripture is often difficult to understand and easily misunderstood.

The Christian Bible writes that Mr. and Mrs. Adam and Eve sinned, so God dismissed them from the Garden of Eden and had to work hard to make a living. Mr. and Mrs. Adam Eve's descendants also continued to commit crimes, so God destroyed all but one family of Noah, who survived with each pair of animals.

But they also continue to sin, which is called the original sin of Adam- Eve's lineage.

Although the Bible does not talk about the fact that there is a Paradise garden other than Eden and whether there are any other families, however, based on the principle of Dualism in Creation, the existence of many Eden gardens and many families like Mr. and Mrs. Adam Eve is possible if not inevitable. Those families have made no mistakes, so they continue to live in the perfect, happy Paradise of the Metaphysical World or Invisible/Formless or Supernatural World (MW). Those families do not represent human ancestors. In other words, Mr. and Mrs. Adam Eve's family is a sinful family, while non-sinful families should not be kicked out of Heaven.

According to Buddhism, thoughts create the Universe. Mindfulness creates a formless metaphysical world. Mistakes in thinking are called False thoughts that create this tangible world. This delusion is caused by the sins of sentient beings.

So, according to the two Major Religions, God built the human world, but because of errors in the process, suffering occurred. This mistake is absolutely not the Creator's (who is omniscient and therefore is never wrong). The Bible wrote that it was because the snake seduced Mr. and Mrs. Adam Eve to eat the Fruit of Knowledge /Discrimination, prone to death (Death is caused by the loss of the noumenon of EM that is permanent, homogenous, timeless and spaceless). Buddha said it was due to the Original Mind being neither right nor wrong, but mistakenly believed that it is always right, similar to Mr. and Mrs. Adam Eve mistakenly believing that any fruit humans eat will give people eternal life. Therefore, the laborious exercise and endurance of sufferance are the path of practice to correct the error of those in Creation who have False thoughts (or eat forbidden fruits), giving rise to a Mind of discrimination. The sin is nothing but the loss of the Non-discriminative Mind of the EM.

Matthew 7:13-14, *The Narrow and Wide Gates*
[13] "*Enter through the narrow gate. For wide is the gate and broad is the road that leads to destruction, and many enter through it.* [14] *But small is the gate and narrow the road that leads to life, and only a few find it.*

I. PLEASURE AND PAIN: THE LAW OF THE WORLD OF DUALITY

Pleasure and suffering, like the ebb and flow of the tides, are two opposite states of life that everyone experiences in this physical world, maintaining a delicate balance.

As an absolute rule, in this physical world, no one can enjoy joy without suffering preceding or following sorrow. So people often want two words to win (win-win) to express the desire to win again after this victory, but no one in life wins for life. The reason is that life is always changing up and down like a sinusoid line.

When observing, that is, dividing an object into two parts, temporarily called the Yin (Negativity) and the Yang (Positivity). With an insight into the meaning of this concept, life is a whole being that two mutually attached antitheses can simplify: if there is a Yin, there must be a Yang, and there can be no whole being consisting only of the one without the other Yin or Yang. The sentient considers him a wholeness, each of whom has his Soul and body. A common mistake in the concept of binary is the lack of recognition of the almost universal imbalance between Yin and Yang according to the disproportionate principle of all objects in the Universe. The objects are all different, so some sentients have a lot of positive or, on the contrary, a lot of negative. Therefore, it is possible to say that males have more positive than negative phenomena and females have more negative phenomena.

To summarize, the law of pleasure and pain is the law of this dualistic world. The exception to this rule is that in the Ultimate Realm (oneness, Realm of the Truth, Goodness, and Beauty), there is only happiness and Heavenly goodness, which will be discussed later.

Return to the laws of the dualistic world of pleasure and suffering, pleasure and suffering are not balanced in everyone: some people are momentarily happy, others are suffering. In short, in the dualistic world, suffering is obligatory. The following is to explore which mechanisms cause a lot of pain or joy from the perspective of science and religion.

II. THE SCIENCE OF PLEASURE-HAPPINESS AND PAIN-
A. SCIENCE OF PAIN AND PLEASURE

PAIN AND PLEASURE belong to the cognitive part for sensations that are obtained from (1) Form (peripheral information), (2) Perception (reception in the peripheral nerve transmitted into the brain), (3) Feeling (causing initial sensation and instantaneous reflexes [commonly referred to as unconditional reflexes, e.g. knee reflexes or closing your eyes when you suddenly see a strange object flying into the eyes]) (4,5) Transform and Integration (of the information after entering the brain and generation of Consciousness/emotion by comparison with the pre-existing Consciousness and ultimately referral to the Omniscient /Original Mind).

The above five processes are carried out in a process called the five Skandhas that form the wholeness of humans: The form represents the physical body, and the remaining four components form the metaphysical aspect of the human. The above process ultimately connects the newly received information into the different brain regions and the internal/emotional brain regions. After the integration, the information is compared with the information already stored in the Inner Consciousness (CS)/Emotional component. In creatures with brains, most of the content consists of the Default Network; in the Beings of the MW without brain, the content is stored in the Soul). This final process has the task of comparing new information with stored information: new information is like stored information that delights; this new information is labeled as feeling joyful; new information is like stored information that suffers; this new information is labeled as feeling pain.

The information of grief or joy ultimately triggers the gray matter of the brain. They consist of the gray matter of the automatic sympathetic or parasympathetic systems, the gray nuclei that make neurotransmitter chemicals, and the cerebral cortex that moves part or whole body to express feelings to the person in contact (Fig F1). Thus, emotion is different from non-emotional CS by the fact that emotion is expressed by physical appearance and different movements. Nonaffective Consciousness is represented in language and action or is not expressed externally and is only used as an inner Consciousness model for future information. .

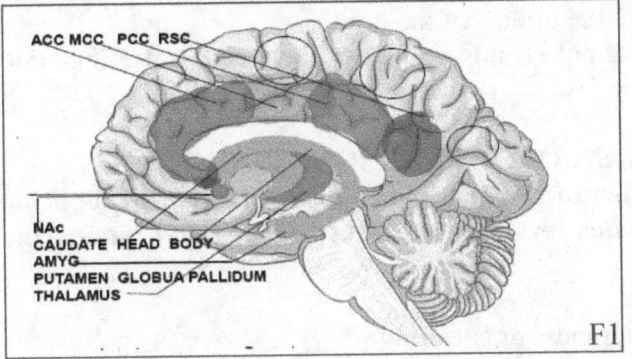

F1

The gray nuclei have a prominent role in the knowledge of joy as the nucleus NAc/ventral Striatum...., fear or anger as AMYGD. Other brain regions, such as ACC and PCC, also contribute to the emotion. The above structure demonstrates that a feeling of joy or sadness has been installed or wired in the brain. Appropriate information will stimulate the center of pleasure or sadness, anger or love after the data is checked in the inner emotion component.

Feeling pain and CS that have blocking features cause grief. The feeling of joy and CS that has favoring or facilitating features cause pleasure. More generally, all factors that cause the stalemate make misery, and any benefit makes pleasure. So, in reality, joy and sorrow are admixed in no order according to the law of chaos and the Entropy (degree of chaos) of the Universe. So, there is also joy or sorrow in pain or joy.

Suffering and joy are feelings that often arise during and immediately after an event. The long-lasting feeling that survives after suffering or joy is called Depression and Happiness.

B. HAPPINESS AND DEPRESSION/MELANCHOLY
They are two parts of the long-lasting emotion. Unlike suffering and pleasure, depression or Happiness is not in the course of events but a long-lasting psychological state after events. This suggests that this type of emotion takes time for the brain to gather a lot of information together to give a feeling of depression or

Happiness. This phenomenon is evidenced when a depressed person is treated with antidepressants. The patient needs a week or two to experience the effects of the drug.

Affliction is mental status bridging between suffering and depression

C. THE MECHANISM OF EMOTION.

Emotions are part of the Consciousness expressed through the automatic nervous system, gestures, voice, and endocrine system.

and depends on

i. Source of Happiness or suffering

ii. The structures of the sensory organs and the structures of the brain that make the initial sense of unconditional, immediate response

iii. CS and emotion. Because CS and emotion depend on;

a) Inherited genetic traits from parents.

b) The living environment. Because the Consciousness and the inner feelings are formed and developed to make the emotional pattern necessary for comparison with new feelings to integrate. Therefore, the school and social family environment plays a weaker role in the feeling of Happiness and suffering.

c) Diseases of the brain, for example, in the vmPFC area, as in the typical instance of Gage Phineas. He was injured in the vmPFC area, showing that after his injury in the vmPFC, his morality changed; he became *antisocial* with a lack of empathy. Compared to before he was injured, Phineas was one of the most prominently sympathetic men in his workplace. The story speaks that after being injured, you have taken away the people you had before being injured.

So, the sense of pleasure or suffering depends significantly on each individual's general state and condition, in which the genetic and past mental development includes family, education, and society. The following elements form the CS pattern and emotional pattern for each person. For the same event or problem, each person's immediate reaction and long-term affection develop differently. For the same event, one prefers the other hates. For leftists, one considers the fact to be a blunder; the other considers it an education emanating from love. As mentioned above, the above difference is due to the emotional part of the model.

Philosophers have long observed that Happiness, as well as Depression, develops from mechanisms that come from within, of course from the Soul, based on the CS. These are two opposites but disproportionate. In the world of the human race, it is predominant. In the world of Paradise, there is no suffering. Also, long-lasting Happiness in this physical world is very difficult to find because pain always intersects. Heaven is at a low level; there are more joyful than painful feelings and more Happiness, so there is less depression.

In his book The Happiness Hypothesis (2006), Jonathan Haidt thinks that this world is dualistic, so Happiness is a matter of the balance of interior and exterior. It should be said that Happiness may have some heart from the outside world. For example, using money for the poor can contribute to Happiness. This way of finding Happiness is an ingenious desire for ourselves to lack morality in love or love. Again, it helps you to hear that it brings joy but not Happiness. Because joy is a momentary moment, the inner Mind is not easily altered by a momentary act, but it takes longer for the brain to adjust. But regret instead of suffering often or entering into everyday life makes Happiness fragile. In summary, Haidt's idea is not based on the long-term barriers to Happiness and depression, which is hard to convince.

III. SCIENCE

Over the past two centuries, man has made significant progress in understanding the Universe and nature. Einstein's theory of relativity and NASA's James Webb Space Telescope (JWST) have opened up a broad vision of the Universe of billions of celestials. Some scientific achievements are in Electronic microscopy, chemistry, and biology with molecular analysis techniques, as well as CERN's Large Hadron Collider, which breaks hadron particles in the nucleus of an atom into measurable Quantum particles. In summary, scientific advances have allowed humans to look far into the Universe for billions of years, up to 300 million years after the Big Bang (compared to the age of the Universe of 13.8 billion years), measuring small energies up to $6.6260701510-34$ joule-hertz (or Joule-seconds), identifying small Photon particles up to zero weight and the speed of light 300,000km/s.

On the other hand, in the metaphysical world described in the classics, the major religions often refer to incomprehensible phenomena to CS and science. The above fact can be expressed by two typical phenomena to be studied and explained in the following sections of this book on the mechanism of following two typical phenomena: Supraluminal speed of light and Miracle

So, what is science capable of achieving such results?
According to Wikipedia, science is a system of CS based on proven and predictable theories about the Universe. In the above definition, it is necessary to clarify the meaning of CS
Consciousness /CS is the understanding of the state inside (in the body) and outside (of course, the Universe) in the awakening state of the brain.

The brain is an important part of the receptive nervous system for transforming information into CS (after the five processes of Mindfulness called five Skandha in Buddhism) as presented earlier: The brain is a useful information filter because thanks to the brain, information can become commands for movement and as a means to communicate with humans and nature through CS. (But the Soul /also called Karmic CS of sentients without physical body can directly contact the Person or other Souls to convey information.) The brain is the intermediary between CS and data. The brain is an information filter. This filter often deviates information that becomes unique to each individual and obscures much information as it is. The Buddha called it the veil of ignorance. Therefore, CS is always information not as it is. CS is not true information because data from the brain is limited and can be distorted and become an illusion. Buddha said CS is the reflection of the veil of Ignorance or simply CS is a product of ignorance. Knowing that Ignorant is not unintelligent but ignorance represents a limitation of CS within the range of senses and machines, including because artificial Intelligence is still a product of CS and sensory organs. Opposing with Intelligence is stupidity or ignorance (as seen in an animal) (Fig F2)

Thanks to the relentless pursuit of knowledge through science, Neuroscience has made significant strides in understanding the neural mechanisms behind emotions such as suffering, depression, joy, and happiness. However, science, being a human endeavor, is not without its limitations. Despite our best efforts, the fundamental question of why humans endure such profound suffering in this world remains unanswered, serving as a testament to the complexity of the human condition.

IV. THE TAO OF HAPPINESS AND DEPRESSION
A. WHAT IS THE TAO?

MORALITY is a spiritual theme that is commonly known in society. This is a combination of TAO and its manifestation - What is TAO? Tao indicates the journey. However, the ultimate feature of the journey must be a starting point. The initiation point is essential to understand all manifestations and possibilities of the journey. In Lao Tsu's Tao Te Ching, TAO is referred to as the absolute beginning. By knowing the root or the ultimate cause of the event or by understanding the mechanism of a process, one can understand and predict the phenomena already occurring and, even when they have not occurred yet. Absolute origin is a concept that cannot be expressed or known through speech or CS. The temporary name of this perfect origin is the Creator (God), the Emptiness/ EM, the Original Mind (other than the Self), the Holy Spirit, the Buddha, and Jesus. This is unperishable (No death, No Birth), Omnipotent, Omniscient, Omnipresent, the Lord of all things. Other attributes are wisdom/all-awareness, ultimate power, infinite cleverness, unmeasurable kindness, unmeasurable loving, and miracle. - Morality is a phenomenon that is the manifestation of TAO so that it can be recognized through knowledge, and expression.

So, to understand the core of any trouble, TAO can be the answer. The spiritual understanding of TAO is characteristically original in the understanding mechanism of the development of the phenomenon. What about the reason for that? That's because TAO in the major religions is the revelation/discovery of the religious Master about the origin of the Universe Creation. In Buddhism,

Buddha knows this Creation through Meditation. In Meditation, the information received is like a vision. The reason is that at a high-level/fourth-tier meditation, the brain is considered an information filter that no longer has the ability to block information.

The distinctive difference between the Revelation of the major religion and the science- theory of philosophers and scientists represent the products of the brain/filtering membrane/or the Ignorance veil. The evidence is that the theories of philosophers or scientists always change with time (old-now) and space (e.g., East-West). On the contrary, the revelation in the major religion has not changed. Know that the scriptures in the religion may not reflect the true essence of TAO. It is not to mention that there are often defects and errors in the transcribing and understanding of the scriptures. Therefore, although He had been proclaiming the dharma for 45 years, Buddha knew that He had not spoken all that He knew, so the Buddha said that in 45 years, He had not spoken a word because language could not be fully described, and disciples could not completely understand language.

In the Buddhist Sutra, Buddha said: "I say things that they do not understand, so I lie. But when they understand, I speak, and so I do not lie."

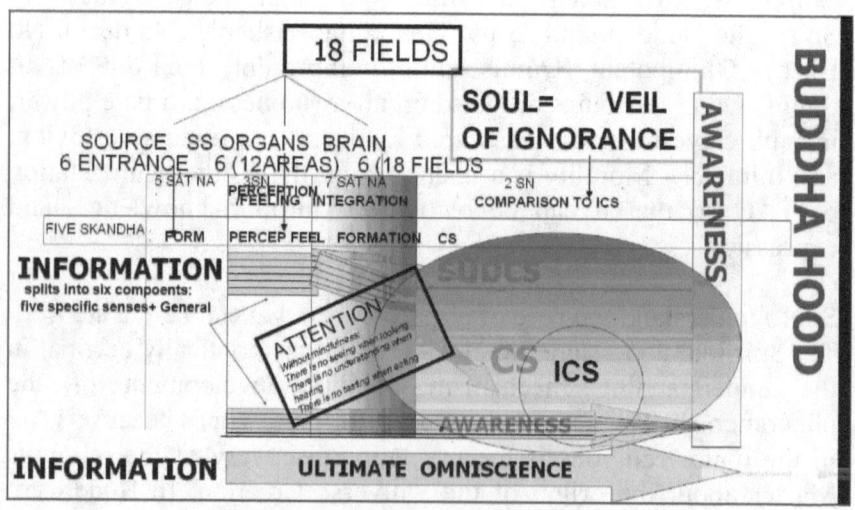

> *F2. The diagram indicates:*
> (Note: Without ATTENTION ☐ Without Mindfulness:
>   There is no seeing when looking
>   There is no understanding when hearing
>   There is no tasting when eating
> Diagram showing the original package of input information undergoing two types of modification:
> - Splitting the original package of information into six types of information: five specific sensory organ types and a nonspecific type
> - Filtering effects by five filters
>   - Milieu (forming six entrances)
>   - Sensory organs (Twelve ayatana, the fusion consisting of six entrance+ six sense data)
>   - Feeling: Information triggers a reflex of defense by using the dorsal pathway
>   - Formation: integration of information by using the Ventral pathway (Eighteen Fields or realm, the fusion consisting of twelve ayatana+ six types of formation)
>   - Consciousness formation by comparing the information in the Ventral pathway to that in the ICS
>
> Therefore, the information undergoes 18 types of filtration called eighteen realms (constituting four steps of filtration) that modify and distort the input. The last step is comparing the data stored in the ICS to label the CS. In the stage of formation, the critical factor is Attention. In the CS labeling, the connection of the ICS with the Ultimate Omniscince/Buddhahood is essential.
>   In the Formation of Awareness, the original package of information also undergoes splitting into six types. Attention is also necessary, but Attention covers large areas.
>   The brain and Attention are unnecessary for Ultimate Omniscience, and the information package is not split. Buddhahood is universal, present everywhere and at any time
>   Without Attention, information is retained in the ICS as SUB CS or UNCS that may exert influence in the functions of viscera and Formation of CS

In summary, Tao is the source of discovery, as Einstein said: Religion without Sscience is blind, Science without Religion is lame. Moreover, today, with computer technology, Science makes social-human beings insane, world wars destroying collective life and politic ghost-like.

PHILOSOPHY OF HAPPINESS AND SUFFERING

Most philosophers correlate life with the desire for happiness and the reduction of suffering.

B. FAR EASTERN PHILOSOPHY
1. I CHING or Book of Change

The book describes nature or any living creature with an upbeat sign that symbolizes two different parts of an individual when observed (i.e., the binary division, represented by Yin/Negative _ _ and Yang/Positive ___). The observation is executed and influenced by the observer. Since the observer is an essential factor, the negative _ _ or positive ___ line should be added to the combination. It is possible to represent each individual or entity in nature by correlating the combination of three lines in any order. As a result, there are eight different types of combinations. After all, one uses three lines to express an individual, which is called the triagram. In society or nature, there is an interrelationship with each other. To symbolize this interrelationship, two trigrams are combined into a hexagram symbol. The final result was 64 different cases called 64 hexagrams. Because of the mathematical nature of the arrangement of the lines, the association of the observer, and the association of the trigrams/individuals, the 64 hexagrams can be used to express the different states of nature, collective or individual. In each hexagram, there are six lines, each representing the individual's status at each time for 12 x 2 hours per day, 12 months per year. This does not yet mention the age of each individual. The representative symbol has the variation countless times to correspond to the different statuses of conditions that can be encountered.

The most common application is to predict the condition of each person when the person who needs to be predicted tries to harmonize with the condition when the hexagram occurs. Harmony is a condition in which one can symbolize oneself as the wholeness of Nature in the concept that each individual in the Universe is similar and identical to Nature. So, the 64 hexagrams are the general expression of the Universe or human.

Of the 64 hexagrams, 14 corresponded to suffering or stagnation. Likewise, do the adjacent or opposite 14 hexagrams correspond to pleasure and benefit? "... Because the 64 hexagrams represent the different phenomena of nature, suffering or pleasure depends on each individual choosing suffering or pleasure

28 Hexagrams

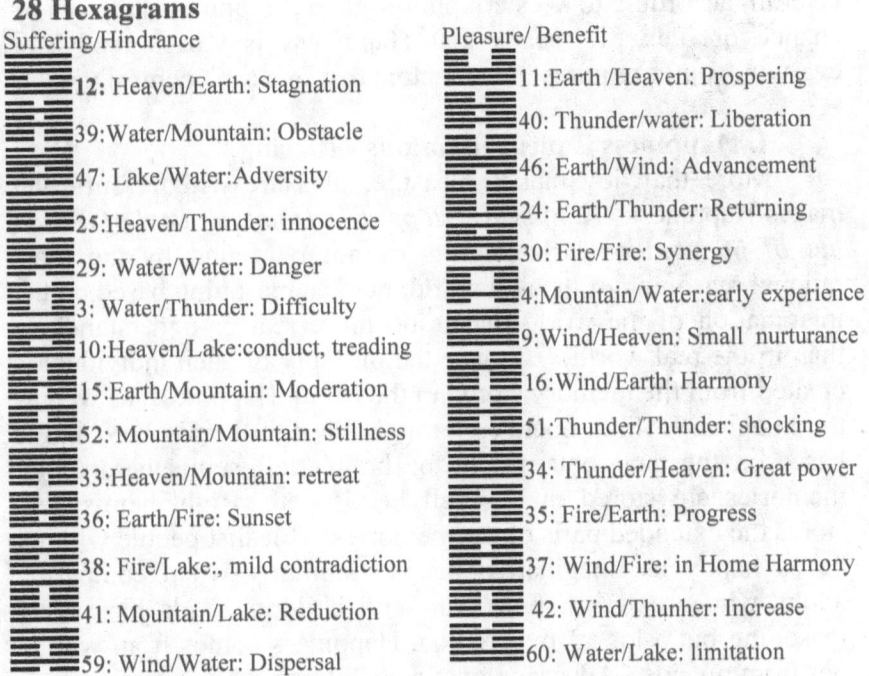

Suffering/Hindrance
- 12: Heaven/Earth: Stagnation
- 39: Water/Mountain: Obstacle
- 47: Lake/Water: Adversity
- 25: Heaven/Thunder: innocence
- 29: Water/Water: Danger
- 3: Water/Thunder: Difficulty
- 10: Heaven/Lake: conduct, treading
- 15: Earth/Mountain: Moderation
- 52: Mountain/Mountain: Stillness
- 33: Heaven/Mountain: retreat
- 36: Earth/Fire: Sunset
- 38: Fire/Lake:, mild contradiction
- 41: Mountain/Lake: Reduction
- 59: Wind/Water: Dispersal

Pleasure/ Benefit
- 11: Earth /Heaven: Prospering
- 40: Thunder/water: Liberation
- 46: Earth/Wind: Advancement
- 24: Earth/Thunder: Returning
- 30: Fire/Fire: Synergy
- 4: Mountain/Water: early experience
- 9: Wind/Heaven: Small nurturance
- 16: Wind/Earth: Harmony
- 51: Thunder/Thunder: shocking
- 34: Thunder/Heaven: Great power
- 35: Fire/Earth: Progress
- 37: Wind/Fire: in Home Harmony
- 42: Wind/Thunher: Increase
- 60: Water/Lake: limitation

2. Far Eastern philosophers.

Far Eastern philosophy is heavily influenced by the I Ching. Death or any hindrances referred to as suffering are not considered unusual problems in life. Maybe philosophers all thought that obstacles in life are as frequent as ordinary laws, as everyday events and obstacles for humans to try to overcome. So suffering is a fact of the life course that has no origin, although when suffering people often mourn "God," Nguyen Du, a famous Vietnamese poet wrote:

In contemplation, every problem in life originates from Heaven Because Heaven forces humans to have the body,

Or when the poet adapts to the Buddhist Dharma about the Karma *"Don't blame Heaven, too."*

Lao Tsu said, *"I suffer because I have that body.*

Loa Tsu is a philosopher who does not discuss death and after death. Know that there is no physical body in the world of Hungry Ghosts or Hell, but suffering is perpetual.

C. WESTERN PHILOSOPHERS

Overall, according to Western philosophers, Happiness happens by chance or luck. It means that Happiness is what's ready for everyone, but it requires many factors that one can't control yet.

1. Happiness is pleasure minus suffering.

More than joy makes pleasure, pleasure without suffering makes Happiness. Kant said, *"Happiness is not an ideal of reason but of imagination"*. (Happiness cannot be found by the most rational reasoning of the real world, but is a reasoning based on the imagination of the world that is no more real or understandable than in the real world). Because the morality of each individual is created from the memory stored in the Mind, Happiness, as well as the imaginary Mind, operates through the right hemisphere and is based on the facts obtained in the brain's left hemisphere. (note: memories are stored in the Left hemisphere, Right hemisphere stores the extended parts of the memories). Idealist people will not be as happy as imaginative people, similarly when comparing adults who are less happy than with children. Kids have little reasoning but a lot of imagination. Happiness comes from within, not from outside. Adults go outside. Children who are less able to experience outside are generally happier

2. Hedonism: Hedonism seeks joy and avoids suffering
Usually it's a material pleasure. From ancient times, there has been the notion that "filling your belly day and night is joy.".

3. The hedonistic Utilitarianism
The pleasure obtained by the right thought and action is, of course, better than Hedonistic Egoism. Hedonistic Egoism is the opposite of Eudaimonia because this kind of Happiness must be obtained in the moral spirit.

4. Psychological/motivational complacency

Self-initiation to seek pleasure is often a failure, so it is more about psychology than theory. The reason is that the Self is always evil while the treasure is higher. Someone said: "*Happiness is like a butterfly; the more you chase it, the more it will elude you, but if you turn your attention to other things, it will come and sit softly on your shoulder.*"– Henry David Thoreau, born in 1817 in Massachusetts

"*The pursuit of Happiness is a toxic value that has long defined our culture. It is self-defeating and misleading. Living well does not mean avoiding suffering; it means suffering for the right reasons. Because if we're going to be forced to suffer by simple existing, we might as well learn how to suffer well.*" -Mark Manson

According to Mark Manson, there is no way to avoid suffering, even living a decent life. On the other hand, being forced to suffer, it is kown as learning to tolerate suffering. Therefore, sufferining is not totally related to the lifestyle but is related to other causes that Marl Manson hasn't understood yet

If Happiness is pleasure minus suffering, then Happiness is only in the world of Heaven. Finding everlasting Happiness in the PW is not realistic.

The ethical or normative model of pleasure is based on the Consciousness of pleasure. So, the pleasure is predetermined. The perception of pleasure depends on society's notion of charity.

5. Pleasure is based on personal
content and axiological values. This concept is similar to value hedonism.

6. Aesthetic pleasure
as Thomas Aquinas proposed, aesthetic pleasure is deeply rooted in theoretical beauty. Kant's explanation that beauty affects the Mind further enlightens us. It's not wrong to say that beauty is akin to intellect and is highly unlikely to be incompatible with ignorance. Creation, based on intelligence and goodness, naturally fascinates man with its beauty and goodness. In the philosophy of Duality, EM creates Power and Omniscience, then Omniscience creates Knowledge and Beauty. **Ignorance and Ugliness only happen by mistake in Creation.**

7. The school of Cyrene,
the predecessor of Aristippus (4th century BC). Happiness is from the inside, including selfishness, encompassing the absence of suffering. Going further, this school does not go deep into the root of the problem; that is, only knowing the phenomenon of the problem gives joy. It isn't very certain about the practical aspect of this above conception. Because the conception of external phenomena lacks depth, it becomes shallow, material, and temporary.

8. Democritus is considered the 'laughing philosopher'
because of his emphasis on the value of 'cheerfulness,' Plato believes that Happiness results from moral effort and acceptance of reality.

9. Aristotle 384-322TTC uses the term eudaimonia to
refer to the Happiness and prosperity that man can attain with morality. Without morality, Happiness is just a personal settlement. It's Happiness at the middle level.

10. Cynicism goes further than suffering and denies Happiness
(Socrates, Antisthenes, Chrysippus, and Epicurus).
Antisthenes) (c. 445 – c. 365 BCE) Xenophon, Diogenes Laërtius: believed to be crazy to seek Happiness

11. Epicurus, Pyrrho,
the meaning of human life is to seek friendship and no pain. Cyrene thinks that life is about seeking peace (ataraxia). They only pay attention to the present because the past has passed and the future has not yet arrived.

12. Augustine of Hippo (354–430)
emphasized the love of God as a source of Happiness (it is not wrong at all, but it does not indicate how to apply it in life).

13. In resurrection time,
Boethius indicates that God is perfect and God is embodied through love. This is very true, but how can love turn into lasting Happiness? On the contrary, it is a sacrificial and

suffering slaughterhouse. Boethius did not indicate that Happiness would not happen in this world, only in Heaven.

14. Philosophers from the Middle Ages also followed Maimonides's belief that Happiness is to seek wisdom
Aquinas finds that Happiness is impossible without going back to God

Al-Ghazali being a mystic and an Islamic philosopher who seeks Happiness by obeying the ritual, is able to resolve and discource evil. There are four things: (i) God Knowing, (ii) Knowing the world around us, and (iii) the future world. And (iv) Transforming the Soul into serving God.

15. Early modern period,
Montaigne argues that Happiness depends on each individual and is unrelated to society.
Bentham's theory of utilitarianism. The ultimate gain is Happiness minus suffering. This way of thinking is wrong because it creates a lot of suffering. However, it appears that Bentham did not know or notice that the event could have good consequences for the future.
Schopenhauer believed that selfishness and love were reality based on ideas about the will to live. The desire is always unlimited, which creates expectations and ultimately causes pain.
Nietzsche argues that pursuing Happiness avoids disgust because it is equivalent to egoism. Therefore, interest is selfish, so weighing on seeking a higher purpose is better than suffering unhappiness.

16. Currently Władysław Tatarkiewicz (1886–1980)
that Happiness is total satisfaction
Herbert Viktor Frankl
(1898–1979) pointed out that in his time, the choice was restricted by the laws of the social pattern established by a few people (authoritarian) rather than by democracy.
Viktor Frankl (1905–1997) believed that unwanted Happiness was achieved by feeling happy with it.
Robert Nozick
(1938–2002) American philosopher criticize hebdomia, utilarism

Michel Onfray
(born 1959) and David Pearce (born 1959) favors atheism and pleasure.

Jean Paul Sartre.
see later.

Western Philosophy can be summarized.into three directions as follows.
i. To find the enjoyment of existence and of opportunity,
ii. The suffering to overcome and seek high spiritual Happiness
iii. Intermediate tendency for Happiness in life is not easy to find

There is a difference in the concept of life: no one in the physical realm, even though living with the above ideas, has full happiness.

C. HAPPINESS AND SUFFERINGS IN RELIGIONS

Unlike science and philosophy, religion has teachings based on the revelation of the Creator/God, who originally created the whole Universe. The information received is intact and as it is (absolute truth [sic]).

The majority of people believe in science and deny religion and spirituality theological power because of the propaganda that science is based on facts, evidence, and the ability to predict accurately. Science denies divinity because divinity is based solely on faith in the revelation of the Buddha, Jesus, and the Old Testament. But think again; science also builds on propositions. Mathematics based on Euclid's proposition reveals many errors with the vast Universe with non-Euclidean geometry. Modern science is based on Einstein's theory of relativity (that Photons have no weight, m=zero, and have an absolute velocity of the light; nothing travels faster than light); science is also based on the "Copenhague's Quantum interpretation" proposed by Bohr of the Netherlands. Bohr and Einstein never agreed on the Quantum world. Saying so shows that science, basically, is also based on "revelation." The difference between the Revelation in Major religion and the science is the revelation of the Buddha or of Bohr and Einstein. When Einstein said that Photons with no weight should travel the fastest, the conclusion was that it was just a proposed proposition with no preamble. Physicists found that the fastest-moving light was true, but it was true only in the field of science and not in religion (note: Science is limited by the veil of Ignorance). The Buddha is omniscient, has a sound Mind, and sees things as they are without deviation from any point of view, even in the physical and metaphysical realms. Buddha moves faster than light or has many activities that are inconsistent with phenomena in physics.

God, Jesus, and Buddha are never wrong (sic) (there is only a misunderstanding of the Testament or Buddhist Sutra by the worldly people), but Einstein and Bohr are occasionally wrong (if there are no mistakes, why do they argue with each other until death and they don't look at each other). At least one person or both are wrong! With the wrong foundation, the outcome is only true within the scope of their proposition; religion and spiritual revelation cannot be denounced.

In summary, the divine authority of religion is only the other part of the entity that science cannot see because of the Ignorance veil of humans from eternity. So science only helps people understand more about emotions but cannot illuminate why people suffer so much as the most undesirable emotion

1. CHRISTIANITY
In Christianity, the Universe, the angels, Satan, even Hell, and man were created by God in one week (celestial time). He created Adam and Eve. But from the beginning of Creation, after the Creation of Heaven and earth, the animal and tree, God created man in the natural environment, with fruit trees to live and to govern the animals. The Bible encourages people to give birth to more, as the Bible says:
Genesis 1:27-30

So God created mankind in his own image, in the image of God, he created them; male and female he created them. [28] *God blessed them and said to them, "Be fruitful and increase in number; fill the earth and subdue it. Rule over the fish in the sea and the birds in the sky and over every living creature that moves on the ground."* [29] *Then God said, "I give you every seed-bearing plant on the face of the whole earth and every tree that has fruit with seed in it. They will be yours for food.* [30] *And to all the beasts of the earth and all the birds in the sky and all the creatures that move along the ground—everything that has the breath of life in it—I give every green plant for food." And it was so.*

Then, human beings are born with ready food and do not have to work. There is no mention of the word "Suffering." Thus, there is Happiness in the most perfect realm, Heaven. Then the Bible says that Adam and Eve lived happily and did not have to work to feed themself because food was available. But it is a family full of sin: Eve listened to the serpent's words, begging Adam to eat the forbidden fruit, so they began to discern good and bad, loss of homogeneity, and other equality of primacy realm, the Emptiness. Because they did not listen to the commandments, they sinned, ate the forbidden fruit, could no longer live eternal life, and their Mind was not clean, so they were not fit in Heaven. So, they were expelled from Eden and had to work hard to live. This suffering in the Bible is considered a punishment for the original sin of losing quality of the Original Mind. Knowing that differences are not the same but not different is the position of the Foot No/Very/ST. Grandfather's grandchildren are causing more and more sins, hating and killing each other, forcing God to cause a flooding disaster, but God finally helps this family not to exhaust itself.

Although Christianity is studied and commented closely and focuses on the evil and suffering and salvation of the Savior. But their continued suffering has destroyed so much faith. Evidence is that anthropological, atheistic, and existentialistic concepts have developed prosperously. Cruel wars, natural disasters, and genocide have continuously struck us despite the Praying the Lord.

There is a man named Beckmann: "Tell me, God, when has He been kind? Did you show kindness by allowing a bomb to explode the body of my only one-year-old son? Oh, my boy! It was destroyed by a bomb! Maybe you showed kindness when you allowed my son to be murdered? Oh, the goodness of God, are you that?" Many times, people see evil come out naturally with no near cause to understand why. It is a negative perception of man who has no escape from evil. St. Augustine said that evil results from the world's lack of good. The Creation, as a stream, the farther away from the source, the more turbid due to the lack of goodness of the Creator. Evil is not created. But the judgment is also an excuse for why the Lord, the Almighty, does not do goodness more fully! It is said that evil is necessary to make good more prominent and God's authority, but God definitely doesn't need anyone to worship Him to please Him.

b) It argues that God created a world of good and evil so that people learn to avoid evil. This means to say that evil begets good. The theory that is stuck in the Creator establishes evil in the physical world but does not establish evil in Heaven. Evil was not created because of Almighty God, but He never created evil morally/Divine/divine casualties. But there are flaws in creating man. However, the defect in the structural mechanism of the Creation is an unacceptable problem here: for example, in the case of a human not knowing swimming can drown. It's a faulty Creation when the Creator creates humans who don't naturally know how to swim while it creates seas and rivers.

Likewise, St. Thomas Aquinas uses St. Augustine's concept that evil is due to the defect of goodness. There is a lack of natural benefits; for example, humans do not have wings to fly.

Throughout the Bible, the description of suffering is everywhere to highlight the sacrifice of Jesus, the incarnation of the Bible in the human world. This sacrifice is not a direct cleansing of their sins, and it is more difficult for them to believe it is redemption. Why that? For as the Lord Jesus, the embodiment of the Lord of infinite power and infinite wisdom in eternity, He created man and Universe with so many thousands of billions of the world; He did not erase the suffering on this world, as little as this earth, so that His children can enjoy the Happiness. His children who have unshakable faith in Him may now be fulfilled of salvation. On the contrary, most people in pain and prayer continue to suffer. Therefore, it is clear that the Lord does not want to remove all suffering or the obstacles of Happiness, for it is clear that He has no intention of removing the suffering or the obstacles He has created Heaven, earth, Hell beings with a lack of some benefit, he intended to make this lack for many Christian theorists.

Jean-Paul Sartre

Jean-Paul Sartre said that man is imperfect and always in the middle: the desire to seize a firm integrity of personality and the free master of Knowledge. Failure is because the Creator creates beings with Knowledge and the false Selfness. But readers will see in the following sections, man is born with an image of God. This image is the Almighty and All-powerful Mind (called Selfness) of the Creator. But because of the original sin, the original image of God was obliterated.

> Self = Emptiness/Original Mind* (−) Sin
> If the guilt is too great,
> Self = (−) Sin
> Sign (−) refers to negativity, metaphysical realm. To simply the the equation, let use the absolute value as follows
> | Self | = | Sin |
> Emptiness cannot be defined or divided, so only temporary use as 'a little' because emptiness is homogenous so a little is like the whole

But the self is always defective (or sinful) and wants to attain the fruits of the Creator. Therefore, there is always a disproportionate desire and achievement.

2. BUDDHISM

Buddhism is often popularized as the religion of liberation from suffering. Its essential teaching is that life is the ocean of sorrow and passion (when drifting from the sea to the shore, it is not the end of suffering but only the illusion of attaining the blissful land. In fact, after overcoming many challenges, the other shore beyond this one is to be liberated from suffering.
This is expressed through the saying

SUFERRING IS BODHI (LIBERATION).

The Buddha said that if one does not recognize life as suffering, there is no way to get rid of suffering.
The saying is applied to the Duality realm, where the two opposite poles, the positive and negative, are split from a single being, the Ultimate Pole, the ultimate realm. This is because, in Ultimate Pole, there is no suffering. The Ultimate Pole is only associated

with unlimited power, and UO is always accompanied by splendor and happiness.

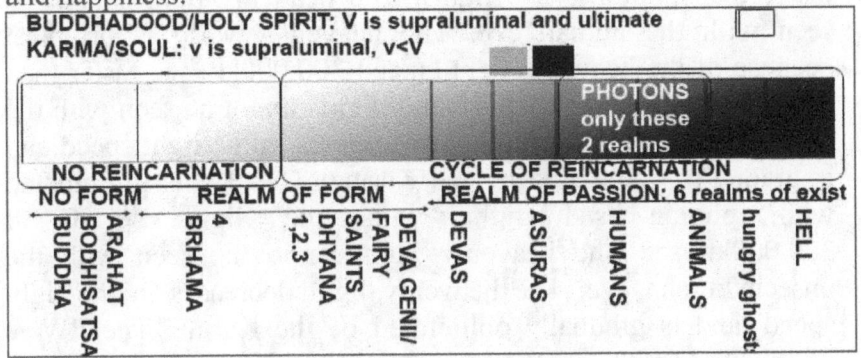

In the realm of Duality, which consists of the realm of Form and Passion together called the Metaphysical World, (Asura, Deva, Saints) are associated with a higher level of spirituality realm than the PW (Humans and animals) and the Invisible Realms of Hungry Ghosts and Hell (see H3). The heavenly world is brightest because of the heavenly light (speed 300,000km/sec faster than photon-based light). The heavenly light cannot be seen with the human eye. The heavenly world is brightest because of the heavenly light (speed 300,000km/sec faster than photon-based light). The heavenly light cannot be seen with the human eye. The heavenly light decreases in the light speed and is gradually obliterated by the Karma. The PW is illuminated with photon-based light with the light speed of 300.000km/sec. The heavenly light cannot be seen with the unseen human eye. The heavenly light decrease in the light speed and is gradually obliterated be the Karma. The PW is illuminated with photon-based light with the light speed of 300.000km/sec. As a result, in the world of hungry ghosts and Hell are dark because the lack of heavenly and photon-based light.

In the realm of Duality, which consists of the realm of Form and Passion together called the Metaphysical World, (Asura, Deva, Saints) are associated with a higher level of spirituality realm than the PW (Humans and animals) and the Invisible Realms of Hungry Ghosts and Hell (see H3). The heavenly world is brightest because of the heavenly light (speed 300,000km/sec faster than photon-based light). The heavenly light cannot be seen with the human eye. The heavenly world is brightest because of the heavenly light (speed 300,000km/sec faster than photon-based light). The heavenly light cannot be seen with the human eye. The heavenly light decreases in the light speed and is gradually obliterated by the Karma. The PW is illuminated with photon-based light with the light speed of 300.000km/sec. The heavenly light cannot be seen with the unseen human eye. The heavenly light decreases in the light speed and is gradually obliterated be the Karma. The PW is illuminated with photon-based light with a light speed of 300.000km/sec. As a result, in the world of hungry ghosts and Hell are dark because of the lack of heavenly and photon-based light.

Buddhist sutra described innumerable worlds at an uncountable distance. In each world, there is the presence of a Buddha with identical Buddhahood who preaches the dharma. For example, Western Land presided by Amitaba, Many Fragrances World presided by Fragrance Accumulated, Wonderful Joy world presided by Akshobhya Buddha Crystal Pearl World by Medicine Master Buddha. Particularly

Vimalakirti sutra cites the world of Many Fragrances world, where living sentients are good in behavior as opposed to humans in this earthly world, who are not well-behaved with stubborn minds. It is necessary for them to apply strict, harsh laws with many extremes, like in Hell. Because of wandering-minded sentients, the peacifying mind needs a more disciplined technique. Therefore, to overcome the afflictions, the Tao practice is going against the common-thinking stream, like navigating against the tumultuous waves of a waterfall

AFFLICTION IS AN ILLUSION.

The Bodhisattva contemplate the world like a magician looking at a magical performance or like a man who looks at the moon in the water or his face in the mirror because the world, magical are what they create, subjective to the rule of birth and destruction and are illusional, conforming with the concept of Dharma is illusional.

In many cases, Mayas are Bodhisattvas who pretend to cause

hindrances and afflictions to reeducate humans. Lotus flowers cannot grow on high-dry soil, only in wet mud. So, the immaterialistic or spiritual dharmas are hard to help humans. The spiritual seeds (to attain enlightenment) cannot grow in tmalae non-discriminatory Emptiness but only develop in the discriminatory, disturbing environment,

Therefore, the management of the affliction is to reduce viciousness and discrepancy by developing compassion, egolessness, four immeasurable minds of virtue, and mindlessness.

---

a) Ten mental models
1. Think of the body; do not pray without suffering, because without suffering, desire is easily generated.
2. Do not pray in life without hindrance, for without hindrance, pride arises.
3. Do not pray without obstacles in spituality, because without obstacles, the Mind is not thoroughly awakened.
4. Build your morality; do not pray not to be disturbed because, without disruption, the will is not persistent.
5. Do not expect to be easy in work, for favorability promote arrogance.
6. Interrelation is not for one's own benefit; for one's own benefit is immoral.
7 Don't expect everything to be according to your will, for your will is the pride.
8. Do not pray for being repaid; for being repaid leads to greed for fame and fortune.
9. see opportunities, don't get into them, for getting into them leads to desire.
10. Injustice does not need justification, for justification leads to attachment.

---

b) Seven Foolishness and Eight Inversions
1,2. Permanent versus Impermanent.
3,4. Pleasure versus Sufferance
5,6. Selfness versus Selflessness.
7,8. Stillness versus Unrest

c) The Four Noble Truths
So when the Buddha walked around the four royal gates, Buddha only saw that the spiritual practitioner was not suffering, so he abandoned the royal palace to follow the teacher.
After proclaiming the first universal sermon concerning suffering, **Dukkha**, for five people as former fellow monks, the Four Noble

Truths, all existence is characterized by suffering and does not bring satisfaction.

the Four Noble Truths are the teaching core, it is:
1. The truth of suffering (Dukkha)
2. The truth of the origin of suffering (Samudāya). The ultimate origin is Ignorance accompanied with the attachment to Greedn Anger , Ignorance, Derision, Stubbornness and Ingratitude.
3. The truth of the cessation of suffering (Nirodha).

Humans in this earthly world have to endure the affliction because the Creator intentionally set up hindrances to human living for reeducation

4. The truth of the path to the cessation of suffering (Magga)

Knowing that the suffering is due to ignorance.

The three most important seal dharma in Buddhist teachings are impermanence, suffering, and false egoism/selflessness.

Buddha said that if life is not recognized as suffering, there is no way to get rid of suffering. Why that? Maybe it's a joy to cover up suffering. According to the Buddha, this is not correct, but it is necessary to know that suffering has a cause; knowing the cause can lead to a way of destroying suffering is the path of cultivation like Buddha.

These Evil Minds increase the other Evil Minds of the Inner CS every day, making it more intense with suppression of the Mind of goodness. The veil of ignorance increases the attachment to greed, anger, and ignorance, resulting in the development of a more evil inner consciousness.

The remedy is the practice of the Noble Eightfold Path, particularly the Right Mindfulness with decent and non-deviated Memory, Right View, Right Thinking, and Right Livelihood.

The Hindrance may be natural due to the setting in the world, society, or the physical body (illness) that causes hindrances to daily life. (Note: in Buddhism, all afflictions are believed secondary to Karma. But in Christianity, when Jesus healed the born blind man and said the affliction was neither the fault of the blind nor that of his parents but was created by the Lord (to teach human).

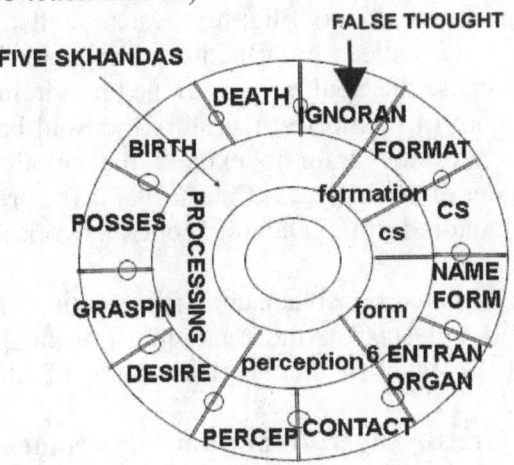

Ignorance initiates the vicious cycle of twelve links of dependency: Ignorance leads to Formation and Consciousness of Afflictions, then leads to Name/Form, Six entrances, Contact and Perception for the creation of Karmas, then leads to Desire, Grasping, Possession for containment of Karma, leading to Cycle of Birth Death then restarting with Ignorance.

In Abdidhamma, taught in the fourth week of enlightenment in Tavatimsa Heaven in its complete form in a single teaching, in the presence of his deceased mother Maya and other Deities, Deva, Buddha pointed out that there are 173 types of Consciousness/Minds including:

121 Mind/Consciousness/Citta composed of
- **67 types of CS**: with 40 Supramundane CS, 27 excellent CS (in Formless [12] and Form [15] spheres),

The above Minds/CS are directly integrated into the sentient Soul; the closer the Soul is to the EM/Buddhahood, the more beautiful and purer the Mind is. This Mind only exists in the MW where

sentients do not have the brain. There is no barrier to the expression of the Mind through emotion
- **54 CS in the Passion sphere:**

These types of Minds are expressed by the Inner CS (Cetasika) through the brain (equivalent to a filtering system/Veil of Ignorance). The process is called by Buddha "Projection". Projection is necessary because the Soul is stuck to the brain in the Default Mode Network/store of memories, therefore the Soul has to use the motor function of the brain to express the emotion (crying, laughing movement of the body, ...) Cetestasika is the pre-existing Mind in the brain stored in the Default Mode Network as memories)

- **24 beautiful CS**/ Kamavaccarasbhanacitta, representing the projection of 24 beautiful Celestasika (the remaining one of 25 Celestska is the Mind to identify the perfect truth of the incomingMind as it is)
- **30 CS of Ignorance, Greed, Anger, Doubtfulness, sleepiness**. (Akusala Cittàna/ Immoral Consciousness) (representing the projection of the Immoral Velestasika) divided into
    12 rooted CS (rooted in attachment, delusions, or ignorance)
    18 non-rooted CS

52 Inner Consciousness/ <u>Cetasika</u>/also called Mental factors, associated with the Mind/Citta,
- 13 Annasamànas / represent Associated or managing factors
- 39 remaining Cetasika composed of

14 Akusala cetasikas, mental factor of Ignorance(Mocatukacetasika/moha) Greed (Lotisetasika) Anger (Docatukacetasita) Doubtfullness (Vicikicchacetasika) Sleepiness(Thidukacetacika)
25 sobhana cetasikas/beautiful mental factors
The 39 "remaining Cetasika plays the role of Inner Consciousness used as a model to identify the new Consciousness. As a result, a new memory triggers the process of integration in the brain with the participation of the Associated or managing factor in the Mental factor/Cetasika). The new data similar to that of at least one of 14 non-beautiful mental factors or akusala cetasikasand 25 Sobhana cetasikas/beautiful mental factors is identify as such that

will activate the correlation centers in the brain for the expression of the emotion.

The above 121 CS represent the phenomenal expression of the Cetasika playing the role of inner CS to trigger appropriate body reaction known as motion

- Note that there is no distinction between the rooted and non-rooted Cetasika as in cases of citta. The reason is the root of Anger, Greed, and ignorance is already present in the Inner CS (Cetasika).

Thus, the feeling of suffering, originating from the 14 non-beautiful mental factors which are affected by the present and previous life, is expressed through the genetic structure of the brain and influenced by the family, school, and society. The Mental factors /Cetasika play an essential role in feeling and expressing feelings. The same situation of challenge varies from the suffering, acceptance or encouragement to overcome for attaining a bright future.

Neuroscience hasn't yet understood the mechanism of conversion of data into Consciousness and emotion. Since F. Crick raised the question of "Neural Correlate of the memories (implicit memory) for nonsensorial general CS is stored in the special part of the brain, the Default Mode Network. However, the conversion into CS is still not completely understood. On the other hand, the Buddhist Sutra with Surangama and Abdidhamma, although not recognized as scientific documents, the mechanism of CS and emotion was revealed more than 25 centuries ago.

The component of the inner CS is very important in Meditation to cleanse the Karma. The clearing of the Karma does not involve the CS, who has the role of expressing feelings. To clear the sin or bad memories, the process has to go deep into the root of the Creation of the MM, which is the Inner CS or Celesika. Teaching, supporting advice, and consoling verbal words exert little consequence on the sins. Contrary to thinking, Meditation is looking in depth at the root of the problem.

In the middle Course Sutra20 *Vtakkasanthàna Sutta* **(KINH AN TRÚ TÀM)**

The Buddha teaches that bad Minds can be expelled from within when focusing on good Minds. The mechanism is like a carpenter using new fine peg to remove old coarse peg. This mechanism is very effective and, of course, practiced in Meditation, repeating the mechanism over many days.

(The above Mind-pacifying technique is similar to that of the First Zen Patriarch, Bodhidharma, whose disciple asked for help pacifying the Mind by replying:" Show me your Mind so I can pacify." Because the Mind doesn't always stop thinking, so He reminds the disciple that the Mind needs attention to fix it; this is not a Koan as some people may think.

Pain, or Affliction, is the setting on this Earth, the dualistic physical world. The problem is evidenced by the fact that a newborn baby always greets the world with crying not laughing:

Being born is crying. Why is it fun not to laugh?
(Poetry of Nguyen Cong Tru)

The baby cries without ever laughing at birth, not just to make the lungs expand out or just the unpleasant environment at birth, but because the mechanism of crying is pre-existing at birth. The unpleasant Cetasika of suffering is available when a newborn. In contrast to the beautiful Mind of pleasure, smile. Laugh, the brain's center for this emotion mechanism develops more slowly in the fourth month of birth. Thus, in the brain, the centers of Greed, Anger, and ungratefulness develop more prominently than the center for morality, loving-kindness, and renunciation.

Thus, spiritual cultivation, especially Meditation, is to repair the Mind, abandon the bad, and enhance the good.

Replacing the evil mind instead of the Good mind can be done with determination at any time. But the most effective time is when the mindfulness in the meditation is attained, because evil mind in the Inner Consciousness is actually identifiable to be replaced by the Good Mind.

It should be noted that one of the three principles of Buddhism is
- Impermanence: the Universe was created from emptiness and must be destroyed
- Selflessness: all things, including living sentients in the Universe, are born from emptiness, so there is no free will; there is an obligation to follow the Creator's morality code.

- Suffering is a problem that is being raised, and this book explores the cause and will point to the cause.

Why have to suffer?   To find the answer or find out:
1. The mechanism of Creation.
2. God's intention to create humans.
3. Why is there suffering that cannot be radically removed?

Chapter II:
THE CREATION OF UNIVERSE WITH SUFFERING

To find out why humans suffer so much, the following is the process of exploring the origins of Creation/Big Bang with the Creation of humans, the Universe, and suffering.

Because the world/Universe was created from Emptiness/EM with the Big Bang or the Creation initiated by the intention, idea, thought of the Creator (also called God). EM has three properties:
1. No birth, no death, or unperishable
2. Self-existence/noumenon or Selfness
3. Oneness, the Creator

EM also has non-discriminative/non-differentiated characteristics, infinite power, and infinite wisdom/Omniscience. From EM, the Universe, according to the concept of "Matter being just the immaterial; the immaterial being just Matter" ("the form being emptiness, and the emptiness being form").

The Metaphysical World/MW consists of Dark Matter (DM) and Dark Force, which comprises 95% of the Universe. Dark Matter, only 27% of the Universe, is unknown to the five senses but has an indirect effect on visible Matter. DM has the gravity that causes the bendinleg of the cosmic grid and thus bends light rays toward Black Matter. (Knowing that Photons do not have weight but are also affected by gravitational force. Photon ray bends according to the cosmic grid. The explanation seems more irrational than scientific to avoid the problem of the zero weight of Photons. Physicists confirm the measurement of non-weight Photons. However, it must be noted that the method of measurement is based on the theory of relativity. Therefore, the measurement is only correct in the setting of the theory but may not be correct in the condition that this theory does not apply. The condition not governed by the theory of relativity is where the particle size falls below the threshold of measurement with the nowadays instruments). The Dark Force is suspiciously accountable for the enormous force that created the Big Bang and the expansion of the Universe. In the world of MW, there are no Photons, no electromagnetic forces, or visible light. But the MW is illuminated with the celestial light, or light of Paradise of God, which is often stronger, more delicate, and more magical in many aspects.

DM can be considered an intermediary between MW and the physical world (PW) because DM is invisible but is associated with gravity that can be measured.

The Soul (Karmic Consciousness/CS) is an entity of Creation. Every entity consists of the visible part and the unseen part. The Soul can be considered an intermediary between the visible world and MW. The Soul may be formed by the DM that belongs to the MW, Neutrino, a small Quantum particle slightly larger than Photons. Both DM and Neutrino penetrate all Matter of the visible world and have features consistent with those known as the Soul. In addition, a Neutrino can be attached to an Electron, which renders the complex having a capability of electromagnetism.

Because of this characteristic structure, the Soul can record information from the visible world and share it with the MW..

Emptiness and MW contain objects that are not visible when using electromagnetic waves. Since the particles in EM and MW are beyond the Quantum level, particles lighter than Photons should travel faster than light.

The following equation involving energy E, speed of light c, speed v, and weight m of the object is only applied to the PW. In this PW, if m of the object is a real number (non-virtual) with v>c, E is a virtual number called Ei

$$E = mc^2 / \sqrt{1 - v^2/c^2}$$

is imaginary number therefore designated Ei.

Because the above equation also belongs to the Universe as well as to the physical world, the virtual energy Ei is not the energy of the object as the objects are real, like Buddha or other sentients in the MW. Therefore, Ei likely represents the Karma (or Karmic force). According to the above equation, the smaller the v gets closer to c, the larger the Karma Ei, and the more it will obliterate the celestial light, and the world becomes dark as in Hell. The following can be used for better understanding: The closer the work is to Buddha's, the faster the v, and the smaller the Karma.

In the PW, Neutrino particles and Photons are the first particles to be created in the Creation before generating other Quantum particles and knowing that Neutrino particles were created before

Photons. The combination of Quantum particles will create visible objects. The visible world was created not only by chance but also by God's Omniscience.

Darwin's study of evolution does not reveal the mechanisms that create the world's suffering. Darwin's theory indicates the formation of the class of creatures, but embryology proves that animals are born directly from God, the father of every creature. Parents only nurse and teach. The Creation of this light is by His will. It may be understandable to say that the Dark Force and DM make up the MW realm that was first born in Creation. Then the PW was born. The above process is consistent with the notion that the Creator first makes the MW. After that, due to the component error in the MW, the PW is made for the sinner. The error in this Creation process is due to error, as the Old Testament says about Mr and Mrs Adam Eve's fault. Buddhist sutras also mention a similar mistake. The Lord never causes mistakes because He is omniscient. After BB, EM ceases to exist and is replaced by Creation, consisting of two worlds, MW and PW.

The intermediate state between EM and Duality Creation is Primordial Duality. This primordial Duality has characteristics such as Nirvana, having space, time, and Matter of the PW

I. THE CREATION OF UNIVERSE AND THE EMOTION.

The search for the origin of the Universe and life is the question of humanity from antiquity. The answer to this question will serve the correctness in establishing behavioral conduct, scientific theories, and philosophical views, ultimately helping to understand why there is so much suffering in life in this world.

All objects in the Universe are born from (1) the Big Bang conceived by Physicists or (2) the False thought of Buddhism, or (3) the Will of God in Christianity. The above three concepts are only to describe an event that originated in this Universe.

A) According to Big Bang Theory (Fig F3)
1. Big Bang

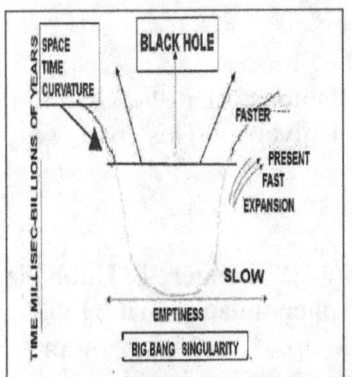

F3

Space-time curvature: time and space curvature, black hole:
Image: The Universe developed after the Big Bang is hypothetically similar to a cone expanding with acceleration without a foreseeable end. For physicists, the end of Big Band may be a Big Rip or Big Chill, Big Crunch with collapse to be restarted with a new Big Bang, or Big Bounce. According to Sir Roger Penrose, with the concept of the black hole having an immense gravitational field, Universe components, when in touch with the Event Horizon of the Blackhole, collapse into a singularity point in the center of the Black hole. This singularity point shares characteristics of the Emptiness of the Singularity of BB

The theory proposed that the Universe starts with one tiny point containing a source of condensed energy, and at a very high temperature, the size of the original may be about 0.1A° or infinitesimally small. The expansion of this point with accelerating speed creates the Universe. The concept can be considered as Big Bang Singularity.

Following the very first moment, there was cosmic inflation (coined by cosmologist Alan Guth, 1980) with the Creation of space and time. After 1/1000 billion sec, the formless energy starts condensing with the successive formation of Photons (particles of Boson type), quarks (meson type), and leptons represented by Electrons and antimatters. A quark is always associated with another quark; particularly, the force of attraction increases with their separation distance.

After $1/10^6$ sec, when the generation of quark came to an end, the quark started to attach to form Hadrons, a proton component without an Electron. The Universe increases in size, is very hot, then gradually cools down. Photons stop their interaction and become light.

Generally speaking, it is divided into two parts.
- Baryonic matter consists of Photons, then the Quantum atomic particles that make up the Universe. This part only occupies 5% of the Universe.
- Non-baryonic matter: Invisible matter 95%

For a few years now, since the JWST entered Hubble's replacement activity, it has shown a phenomenon that Hubble, with a weaker sensitivity, cannot pick up. The vision of more numerous and larger galaxies in about 3-500 million years after Big Bang/BB is an inexplicable fact with the current theory of BB, not to mention the doubt of the expansion of the Universe. These discoveries have surprised and upset many people and led to skepticism that BB actually exists or that theories about BB need to be reviewed.

BB relies on the observation of visible matter consisting of only 5% of the Universe (and not representing the entire Universe consisting of 95% of the invisible part). So any theory of BB may not have a solid reasoning for the assumption of the entire Universe. Again, the religion (Christianity and Buddhism) did not mention this critical event. But maybe the Bible or Buddhist Sutras don't want to reveal it because it's hard to describe BB if BB actually happens.

2. BARYONIC MATTER (MATTER SENSITIVE TO THE SENSES) IN THE PW AND PHYSICAL FORCES

The "visible' (baryonic matter is constituted of Quantum particles that form atoms, molecules, and complex inorganic and organic structures). Quantum particles are all related to Photons. Photons are particles of light and are responsible for the senses' sensitivity of to tthe baryonic matter. In the Old Testament, the Creation of Photons and light corresponds to God's will to create light).

There are about 200 basic particles/matter found in the Universe in Table 1 and Table 2

Further reading Table 1.2: Forces and Matters in Universe.

Six organs of perception	Force/ Form	Particle/ matter	Connecting force	Range	Force
Perceptible, non-emptiness or physical /Form	Weak force,	Quarks, leptons	W,z (decay, radioactive)	Very short	Weak
	Strong force (quarks forming Protons and Neutrons)	Quarks, Gluons binding Quarks	Boson, Gluon (nuclear binding)	Short	Very strong
	Electromagnetis incl Gamma Ry	molec binding)	Photon /Boson(	Infinite	Strong
Non perceptible Emptiness/ Formless	Gravity (mass binding)	mass	Graviton not yet determined	Infinite	Very weak
	Dark Force of 5th Universe force	?	Dark expansion Photons	Infinite	Strong

Bosons: Photon, W+,W-. Z0 Gluon Higgs. and Meson
Fermions: Lepton (Electron, Neutrino…) and Baryons (proton, neutron…
Hadron: Mesons+Baryons

In the PW, there are three forces: electromagnetic, strong and weal forces that is believed to have a common source and can be grouped in one force according to the Grand Unified Theory GUT)

In the MW, there are two forces. However, the gravity force is associated with both visible (measurable, baryonic matter has gravity) and invisible components (because the elementary particles are not yet or cannot be found). The Theory of Everything (TOE) encompasses four forces, including gravity, into one force, which opposes the Dark Force belonging to the MW.

Further reading: Table 1.2 Basic fields seen in the visible Chronology of False thought/ Big Bang) adapted and modified from Google).

Time	Era	Temperature and OM	Characteristics of the Universe
0- 10^{-43} s	Interface (Emptiness-False thought) (Planck Time)	False thought instantly spreading throughout **OM**	Emptiness partially/focally losing its noumenom to produce mulriple infinitely small, infinitely dense Primeval fireball ,with Supergravity as force
10^{-43} s	Big Bang	infinite 10^{32} K, **OM**	described by physics and conceived in spirituality: Dark Force, DM, gravity, GUT/ Grand Unified Theory hyothelically composed of weak, electromagnetic, and strong forces),
10^{-35} s	End of GUT	10^{27} K	Dark Force, DM, gravity, strong nuclear, electroweak Quarks and leptons form
10^{-35} to 10^{-33} s	Inflation	10^{27} K, **OM**	Size of the Universe drastically increased, by factor of 10^{30} to 10^{40} , DM
10^{-12} s	End of unified forces	10^{15} K, **OM**	Dark Force, DM, 4 forces, protons and neutrons forming from quarks,
10^{-7} s	Heavy Particle	10^{14} K, **OM**	Dark Force, DM, proton, neutron production in full swing
10^{-4} s	Light particle	10^{12} K	Dark Force, DM, Electrons and positrons
#100 s	Nucleosynthesis era	10^9 - 10^7 K, **OM**	Dark Force, DM, helium, deuterium, and a few other elements form
380,000 years	Recombination (Decoupling)	3000 K, **OM**	Dark Force, DM, Matter and radiation separate End of radiation domination, start of matter domination o
500 million yrs	Galaxy formation	10 K, **OM**	Dark Force, DM, galaxies and other large structures form in the Universe
14 billion y	Now	3 K, **OM**	Present time

OM: Original Omniescience, DM: Dark Matter

3. NEUTRINO

In 1930, Pauli Wolfgang suspected that the Neutrino was another not yet identified in the Universe, based on the hypothesis of the structure of a proton that is composed of neutron and Electron as shown in the following reaction:

n → p + e + v (p: proton, n: neutron, e: Electron, v: is the hidden number to balance the equation) Neutrino was discovered and confirmed in 1998).

Neutrino is a very light elementary particle without an electric charge, so it does not create electrical fields. The particle is the most produced in the Universe, but because it does not react with other matter, Neutrino is difficult to study, Neutrino can penetrate other materials. AntiNeutrino is no different from Neutrino. Neutrino has an energy of 0.32 eV and is as light as 1/108 of the Electron. Therefore, Neutrino also has gravitational force and has a fast speed that is almost equivalent to the speed of light because it is very light. Neutrino is almost like an Electron because it does not relate to the strong nuclear force like the atomic bomb. However, Neutrinos and Electrons are associated with weak nuclear force. Because of this connection, Muon and Tau counties are also included in this group. Electron, Muon, and Tau often combine with Neutrino to form Electron - Neutrino, Muon - Neutrino and Tau - Neutrino and Antimatter Electron - AntiNeutrino.

Neutrino is present in the first second after the Big Bang, 10-4 seconds. (H1.4) and continue to be born from the planets, and the Earth may be the most particulate.

It passes through all matter, including the body and Earth, without causing a reaction...

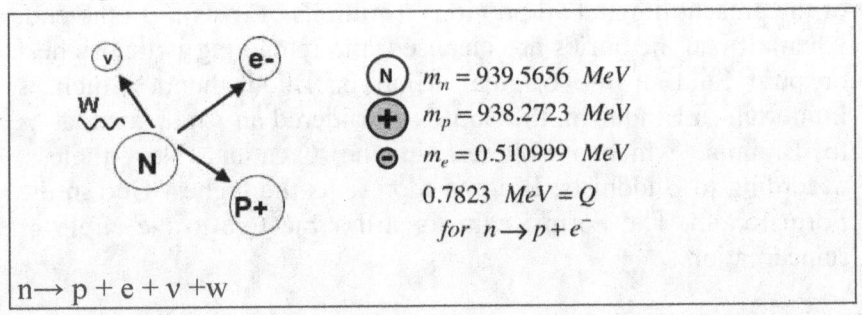

H1.4 Chart indicates neutron particles (N) formed as proton particles (p+), Electron particles (e-) and Neutrino particles (v)

B. THE CREATION OF THE INVISIBLE MATTER (NON-BARYONIC MATTER)

BB or God's will of Creation of the Universe/or False thought activate a change of Emptiness into the present Universe that includes
the visible matter is listed in Table 1.1 and
MW may include Dark Matter, which accounts for 27% of the Universe, and Dark Force, which accounts for 68%.

B. THE SOUL: AN INTERMEDIATE ENTITY BETWEEN THE METAPHYSICAL AND PHYSICAL REALMS.

(SOUL=Karmic Consciousness=Mind vn: Nghiệp thức=HỒN).

Of interest, if the Soul is defined as a microsmos, an analogous counterpart of the macrosmos of the ultimate Deity such as Brhama, this type of Soul does not exist according to Bhuddha. Because Buddhahood consists only of EM/Ultimate or Original Omniscience (OM), whereas Earthly Sentient's Souls consist of Karma /Consciousness attached to OM.

Along with the physical and Metaphysical realm, the Soul is also created from the world.
Consciousness is predominantly the invisible part of living sentients and is the main constituent of the Soul. According to Buddhism, the Soul is not immortal but exists longer than the body and represents Karma, the summation of semantic memories of the present life and all previous (millions of lives). In the end, when all bad memories are cleansed, the remaining is the highest or pure Soul or the original Mind or Buddhahood, which is immortal. In Hinduism, the Soul is considered an Atma, analogous to Brahma, which is highest in the Creation. Nevertheless, according to Buddhists, Brahma represents the highest God in the Form Realm. The Form Realm is still subjective to the circle of reincarnation..

1. IS THE SOUL A REALITY OR NOT?

This is a fundamental problem because no one sees or captures the Soul. Therefore, atheists or existentialists do not accept that they have a Soul, although they still use the word Soul at their disposal!

In addition to the above convenience, many events and phenomena suggest that the Soul exists. This is based on phenomenology.

Based on ontology, all things exist in their wholeness, but humans only perceive a part of this wholeness . Emmanuel Kant said:
What things tell us, we know it. And, of course, I don't know what things don't tell.
This means that we see things as we think they are (because we often know things before they reveal), not as they are.
The Easterner describe things as the wholeness, represented by the Ultimate Pole, represented by an imaginary circles. When we observe the divide the circle into two parts. Yin (Negative) and Yang (Positive)
,
David Bohm (physicist) also calls things the whole of two orders: Explicate Order consists of known phenomena and Implicate Order is an invisible order.

Such a notion is that the Soul is an entity (noting the 'entity' is used in a relative way because Buddhism says that all things (in this PW) are illusions, "The Mind creates all things', note that Mind=Soul=Consciousness=Knowledge, all are distinct from the original Mind=Holy Spirit=Buddhahood) that the five senses do not directly perceive or create the knowledge (Consciousness), but knowledge is created through the senses and the brain.

The Soul is MM; much of it is MM about the meaning (semantic MM) of essential events in life. This is also the Consciousness (CS) of the present life and all previous lives, called store Consciousness. What is Consciousness? It is information processed by the brain and then recorded into the brain's Inner Consciousness region in the form of MM in the neuronal synapses and then copied onto the Soul. No brain still has CS, for all beings in the Universe have CS, but only humans and animals have brains. Therefore, the brain is not required to produce CS. Still, the brain is necessary for humans and animals to express themselves through action and emotional expression through the sympathetic and parasympathetic systems and gestures. CS is one of the instruments for intercommunication between beings. Therefore, when CS is not recorded or does not exist, it does not mean that a thing does not exist. CS has a poor sensitivity compared to wisdom, so using CS to study the Soul is like "using a firefly to light up the mountain".

It should be noted that the Soul plays not only a copy of CS but also plays a vital role in the recall of MM. Without the Soul, MM cannot be recalled (remember)

In summary, with the overall view, the Soul must exist. Rejection of the Soul is because the senses, often called five insurgents, still restrict humans awareness.

2. COMPONENTS OF THE SOUL

From the above facts, the Soul is almost sure to include:
- The Dark Force so that the Soul can move very fast. It is the main part of EM.
- Dark Matter (DM) gives the Soul weight, which can interact with visible matter, especially the brain. The brain transforms data into CS, distorts data, but helps communication with other creatures in the Universe.
- Neutrinos are attached to the DM of the Soul when the Soul attaches to the brain. Neutrino can be attached to Electrons so the Soul can stick to the neural synapses to record neural changes occurring in memory recording. Thus, with the above, it can be suggested that the Soul is the intermediary between the PW and the MW.
- Ultimate Omniscience (UO) is included in Buddhahood. Awareness and CS have to be based on UO to be functional. CS, therefore, does not need the brain, but the brain, on the contrary, reduces the the CS and awareness. In the process of creating the Universe, UO is essential. There is no need to personalize UO as a Buddha image. CS does not need a brain, and artificial intelligence does not need a brain! (note: Awareness can be distinguished from CS by a large extent but shallow in-depth)
- Memory is the part of the Mind attached to the brain. Memory is more material because it uses a neural connection, a transitional component between invisible and visible realms.

3. The experiment of Dr Duncan McDougall and the Book of "The weigher of Souls

Back to the Experiments by Dr Duncan Mac Dougall in 1901 and by Dr Crooks in the First World War, and the book The Weigher of Souls by André Maurois, it is easily understandable that the Soul is associated with weight due to DM as its main component. The Soul weight depends on the method and timing of measurement (ranging from 21.3 g - -0.17 mg). When the Soul leaves the body, the body may become lighter. Know that besides the brain Soul, there is also a Body Soul (which makes the whole Soul; for example, the Soul associated with the physical body without the brain is responsible for the energy described as Chi/Qi in acupuncture in Chinese Medicine or in martial art and human Electromagnetic field) that can leave the body at different times. Maybe one day it will be more scientifically tested when the experimenters better understand the leaving, re-entry, multiple Souls, and body Soul, not only to study the Soul but also to investigate more about the DM and even the Big Bang.

C. Further reading: PROPOSED HYPOTHESIS OF THE SOUL ARCHITECTURE. (Fig F4,5)

Based on the characteristics of the Soul, the Soul may be constructed with the Dark Force and the DM as the Soul substance onto which attached the Neutrino. The Neutrinos can be attached to the Electrons when entering the living being's brain.

Outside the body, the Soul senses information by changing the arranged structural disposition of the Neutrino.

In the brain, the Electrons are Electronically attached to synapses (that change the electrical potential when the incoming information activates the synapses. The structural disposition of the Neutrinos changes according to the structure of the Electron when it sticks to synapses.

When the MM is recorded, the synaptic membrane becomes negative (-), so Electrons do not stick to synapses. The UO of the Soul can control the event of sticking and separating the Soul from the Synapses.

When the brain stops functioning at the death of the living being, in a death experience or out-of-body experience and hallucinogen administration (that changes the synaptic electricity), the Soul and the synapses lose electrical potential; the Soul separate from the brain and leave the body or regains its properties of non-locality.

Thus, Neutrino may be the particle of the Consciousness and Karma/veil of ignorance. However, Neutrinos do not react with baryonic matter. Still, they do when attached to Electrons that are reactive with baryonic matter, as demonstrated by the effect of CS on the PW. Neutrino is not a particle of UO because UO is more delicate than the CS, and UO only reacts with Baryonic matter by the intermediate of the CS. UO is almost included in Buddhahood.

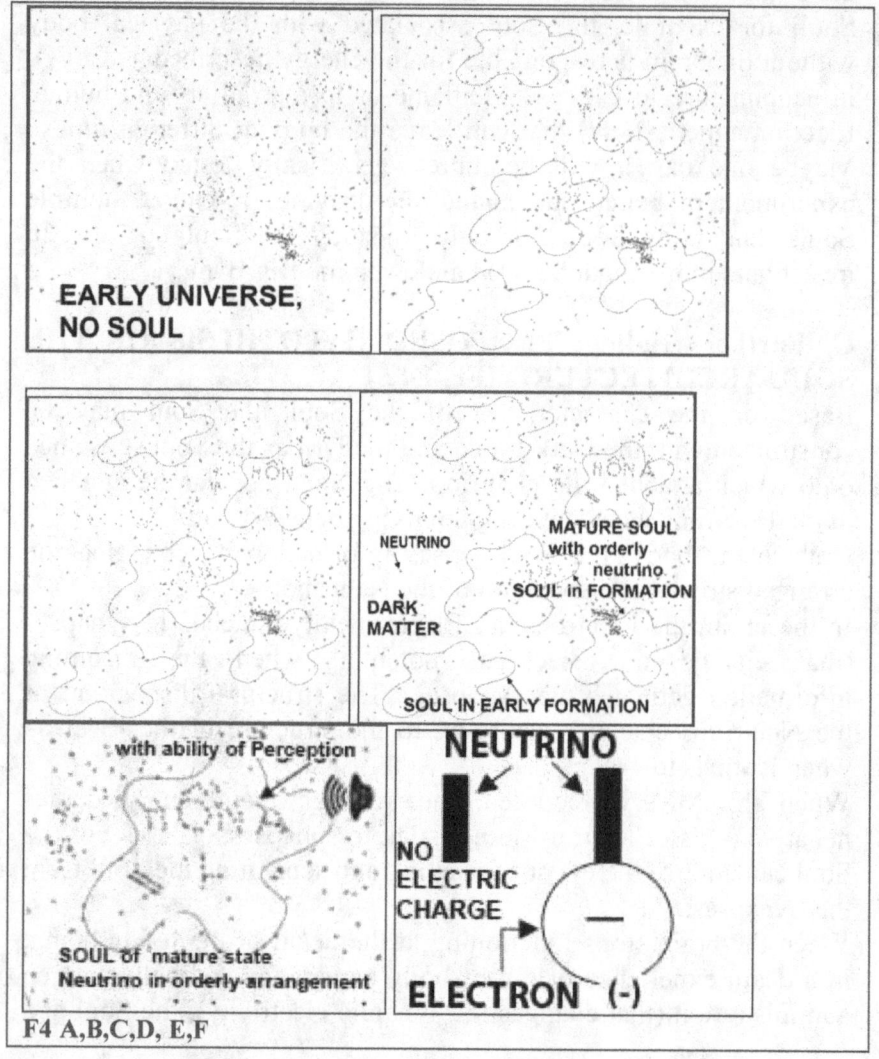

F4 A,B,C,D, E,F

By analogy with Memory Computer Disc composed of billions of transistors (comparable to ON/OFF switches) arranged in many layers to register the electromagnetic changes:

Each particle of Neutrino, with or without attachment with an Electron of a negative charge, renders the Soul to have an electric potential and electromagnetic field. For the information input, light, and sound...) exert momentum on the Neutrino, therefore creating a change in the structure of the Soul. The architecture of the Soul changes with each sentient being.

A: Early Universe with Neutrino, Dark Matter and Dark Force.
B, C: in simple, low-level sentient.
D: higher level sentient.
E: Soul with Neutrino affected by the sound (speaker), without interference of the brain.
F: Neutrino attached by an Electron becoming charged with (-) potential.

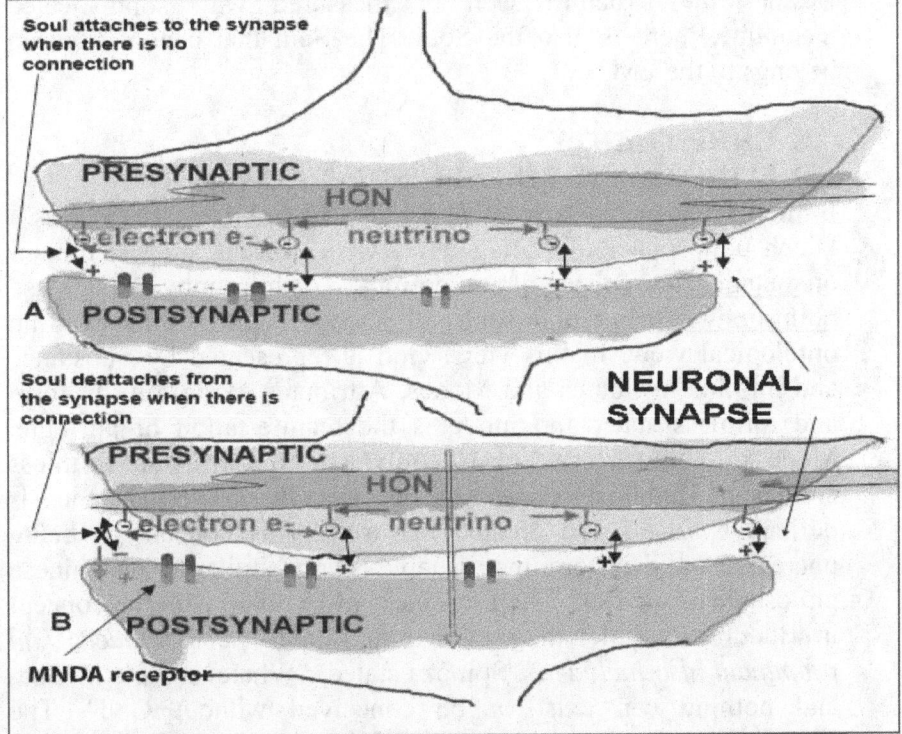

Fig F5 A: Embodied Soul composed of DM and Neutrino attached with Electrons becoming (-) Electronically. Therefore, the Soul can interact with Synapse Electronically, that is, (+).
B: when activated, the Synapse becomes (-), and the Soul is detached. As a result, the (-) charge is created in the Soul.

II. THE EMPTINESS / VOID, VACUUM
A. In PHYSICS.
The vacuum/void is an empty space that does not contain what the sense recognizes. But it has made a lot of people wrong. The Big Bang begins at a point no one can prove except by thought or by theoretical knowledge. The Universe has 95% of space, but it is suspected to contain Dark Force and dark matter that man does not know how to identify. Similarly, the vacuum created in Laboratory of physics may contain Consciousness/knowledge (and thus the vacuum is known as vacuum)

B. In the brain.
Besides the structure seen or measured with sophisticated technique, there is also the Soul. The Soul that cannot be seen belongs to the EM

C. CHRISTIANITY
D. SPINOZA AND METAPHISICAL CONCEPT
Baruch Spinoza (24 November 1632 – 21 February 1677) was a Dutch philosopher of Portuguese Jewish descent, a great thinker on metaphysics, epistemology, political philosophy, ethics, philosophy of Mind philosophy of science. , and religion with an ontological view. In this view, God is represented by Substance and infinite Attributes and Modes. Attributes are infinite in form and formless state, and mode is the manifestation of attribute. Mode in Spinoza concept is equivalent to form and formless entities in Buddhist concept of five skandhas. The substance is defined by itself and created by itself. This concept of being uncreated and therefore imperishable is very similar to the Chinese philosopher Lao Tsu's The Emptiness of Buddha, with the concept in Buddhahood including everything:"*small, not excluded, and prominent also included*". Spinoza stated: "Whatever is, is in God, and nothing can exist or be conceived without God". The Metaphysical Realm, conceived by Spinoza, is very similar to the Universe. Such a concept is contradictory to the current opinion of his time. Therefore, at the age of 23 years, the Talmud Torah congregation of Amsterdam issued a writ of expulsion or ex-communication) against Spinoza.

Spinoza's idea of the emergence of the Universe and God (God) was entirely contrary to contemporary ideas but very close to the philosophers's idea of the Orient. Spinoza identifies God with Substance based on the philosophy of necessity (Necessitarianism) with the principle of sufficient reason (Principle of Sufficient Reason). He denies the accidental existence of Substance in nature. The existence of a substance has many conditions but is summarized in the following three points:
- Every possible Substance necessarily exists.
- Substance is conceived through itself and self-creating/active nature/nurturing nature. Spinoza argues that Substance contains everything in nature (like Buddhism) to solve the problem of the existence of different objects in nature. Without Substance, the above objects cannot exist. The Substance is, therefore, infinite and eternal.
- Every existence has a reason. According to Spinoza, a substance that exists must have a reason, and a substance that does not exist must also have a reason. Going further, the Substance itself is self-generated and self-fruited, and only sufficiently (without excess) is Self-existent.

With this in Mind, Spinoza concluded that only Substance/God is the only possible Substance, and Substance is infinite. The contemporary says there may be more than one Substance. Descartes said there are two substances: the body and the Soul. But for Spinoza, Mind and body are the entities of the Substance.

Probably to address the birth of the Universe, Spinoza proposed the concept of Attribute and Mode. Mode is the expression of the attribute. Substance/God is "need to have," so the Mode arising from Substance/God is also "need to have" and is unlimited (e.g., the Soul, thought, and Universe of the Big Bang are unlimited).

When there is an infinite/unaffirmative entity, there is also an affirmative entity (finite Mode), such as a table or chair. The assertion entity comes from other assertions such as trees, trees... to make a chair table (principle of Duality). The attribute and Mode are equivalent to the grain in Buddha.

Michelangelo's painting of God and Adam

The concept of Substance/God encompasses everything, should address self-existence, and be consistent with the concept of

Buddhism. The image of God that Michelangelo drew may not be in line with the notion that man is the image of God. In it, the image of God as the Holy Spirit is expressed in the Soul of man, not the body of God/God expressed through the physical image of man. God had only the Holy Spirit without the Soul of man at the very beginning; the Holy Spirit had no primal sin due to the separation of Mind. The human body was created by the Creator to temporarily protect the Spirit/Magic and the Spirit for a shorter period of time than the Spirit's life in the world of the Earth/God. Therefore, it is not important for the body.

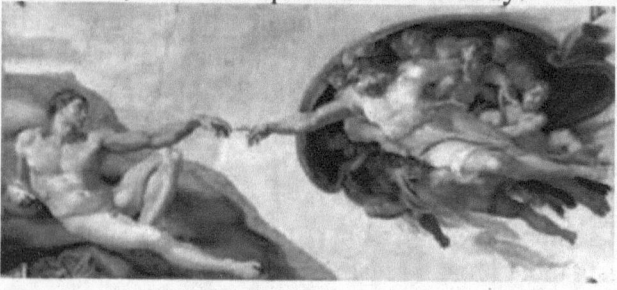

Parmenides (earlier part of the 5th century BCE) said:
" *what exists is uncreated and imperishable, for it is whole and unchanging and complete.*"

III. THE EMPTINESS / VOID, VACUUM.

EM represents the beginning of everything therefore represents Tao

A. EASTERN PHILOSOPHY: THE CONCEPT

Emptiness (vn: Chân Không)/ Tao/ Ultimate pole (vn: Thái Cực) / Original Mind (vn: Bản Tâm)/ are synonyms to designate Buddhahood/ Holy Spirit/ GOD, the ultimate origin of the Universe and all species. Buddhahood/ Holy Spirit possesses immeasurable power, Ultimate Omniscience (UO) (vn: Trí Huệ Bát Nhã), and other attributes like ingeniosity, infinite light, infinite sound, being splendid, homogenous, non-discriminatory, uncreated, imperishable, and not associated with birth or death. Because of the homogeneity and non-discrimination, Emptiness is characterized by the similarity between the microscopic and macroscopic structure in all parts.

Tao is manifested as Taoism or Daoism, which is the way to practice Tao living in balance and harmony with the Universe and ultimately with Tao who creates the Universe. As a result, all discussions of Tao are difficult to express, and the quintessence of the expression in words is difficult to perceive. Lao Tzu (born 571 BC, Chu Dynasty, ancient China) said:
The wise student hears of the Tao and practices it diligently.
The average student hears of theTao and gives it thought now and again.
The foolish student hears of the Tao and laughs loud
If there were no laughter, the Tao would not be it is.

Tao is to take those who have too much to give to those who do not have enough to make the high lower; the low raised. Therefore, Emptiness itself must be filled with content imperceptible to the sensory organs. **Thus, the vacuum per se never exists**. In Taoism, as well as in Major religions and great philosophers' thinking, Emptiness is believed to be the origin of the Universe. Lao Tsu said:
The Tao is like an empty container:
it can never be emptied and can never be filled.
Infinitely deep, it is the source of all things.
…… It is hidden but always present.
I don't know who gave birth to it.
It is older than the concept of God
And
The space between Heaven and Earth is like a bellow;
it is empty yet has not lost its power.
The more it is used, the more it produces;
the more you talk of it, the less you comprehend.
and
Yet mystery and reality emerge from the same source.
This source is called darkness. Darkness is born from darkness.
The beginning of all understanding (Consciousness)
and
When people see things as beautiful,
ugliness is created.
When people see things as good,

evil is created.
And
All creatures in the Universe
return to the point where they began.
Returning to the source is tranquility
because we submit to Heaven's mandate.
Returning to Heaven's mandate is called being constant.
Knowing the constant is called 'enlightenment'.
Not knowing the constant is the source of evil deeds
because we have no roots.

Lao Tsu said
   Look for it, and it can't be seen. Listen for it, and it can't be heard.
   Grasp for it, and it can't be caught.
   These three cannot be further described,
   so we treat them as The One.
   It's highest is not bright. It's depths are not dark.
   Unending, unnameable, it returns to nothingness.
   Formless forms and image less images,
   subtle, beyond all understanding.
   Approach it, and you will not see a beginning;
   follow it, and there will be no end.
   When we grasp the Tao of the ancient ones,
   we can use it to direct our life today.
To know the ancient origin of Tao: this is the beginning of wisdom.

Emptiness (vn: Chân Không)/ Tao/ Ultimate pole (vn: Thái Cực) / Original Mind (vn: Bản Tâm)/ are synonyms to designate Buddhahood/ Holy Spirit/ GOD, the ultimate origin of the Universe and all species. Buddhahood/ Holy Spirit possesses immeasurable power, Ultimate Omniscience (UO) (vn: Trí Huệ Bát Nhã), and other attributes like ingeniosity, infinite light, infinite sound, being splendid, homogenous, non-discriminatory, uncreated, imperishable, and not associated with birth or death. Because of the homogeneity and non-discrimination, Emptiness is characterized by the similarity between the microscopic and macroscopic structure in all parts.

B. HINDUISM /Kena Upanishads

wrote about fullness instead of Emptiness as origin of the Creation: *"From Fullness, fullness comes, when fullness is taken from fullness, fullness still remains."* Similarly Lao Tsu said:*" Approach it, and you will not see a beginning; follow it, and there will be no end.*

C. BUDDHISM

Buddha defined Emptiness by giving an example as follows: when dividing an object into tiny particles, then keep dividing billions of times. The particles become invisible and imperceptible to five sensory organs, becoming Emptiness. It is true because this process's result fits with the Emptiness concept as one can imagine. Therefore, Buddha said Emptiness and Form are not different from each other.

- *Vacuum* **per se** never existed before or after the Big Bang.
- The reverse process (creating Existence from Emptiness) will create the form accessible to the sensory organs.
- The process creating Emptiness from Existence generates energy, similar to making the atomic bomb by splitting atoms.
- Energy must be accompanied by mental processes such as Omniscience, Awareness, or Consciousness because of the principle of Duality: meaning that the process of formation of Emptiness from Existence creates not only the Energy but also the Omniscence, and *that Emptiness is empowered with Energy and Omniscience.*

Therefore, Emptiness, Tao, Buddhahood, and the Holy Spirit are empty but can create Form, Force, and Mind.

Emptiness is static and homogenous, but Universe is not. Therefore, when saying that this Universe is static, Einstein was so embarrassed to correct this.

In the Surangama (kinh Lăng Nghiêm), Buddha said to Ananda
> ...*You should inquire into all the Creations which in this material world are subject to change and destruction. Ananda, which one of them does not decay?*
> *Yet you have never heard that Emptiness can perish.*
> *Why? Because it is not a created thing*

Buddha defined Emptiness by giving an example as follows: when dividing an object into tiny particles, then keep dividing billions of times. The particles become invisible and imperceptible to five sensory organs, becoming Emptiness. It is true because this process's result fits with the Emptiness concept as one can imagine. Therefore, Buddha said Emptiness and Form are not different from each other.

- *Vacuum* **per se** never existed before or after the Big Bang.
- The reverse process (creating Existence from Emptiness) will create the form accessible to the sensory organs.
- The process of creating Emptiness from Existence generates energy, similar to making the atomic bomb by splitting atoms.
- Energy must be accompanied by mental processes such as Omniscience, Awareness, or Consciousness because of the principle of Duality: meaning that the process of formation of Emptiness from Existence creates not only the Energy but also the Omniescence, and *that Emptiness is empowered with Energy and Omniescience.*

Therefore, Emptiness, Tao, Buddhahood, and the Holy Spirit are empty but can create Form, Force, and Mind.

Kena Upanishads wrote about fullness instead of Emptiness as the origin of the Creation: *"From Fullness, fullness comes, when fullness is taken from fullness, fullness still remains."* Similarly Lao Tsu said: *"Approach it, and you will not see a beginning; follow it, and there will be no end.*

IV. EMPTINESS POSTULATE, EMPTINESS AS A POSTULATE, ORIGIN OF UNIVERSE. EMPTINESS IS MIRACULOUSLY EXISTENCE

A. EMPTINESS IS BUDDHAHOOD
Buddhist Sutra.

Buddha said in the following paragraph of Surangama Sutra: if one divides an object such as a block of stone millions of times, the result is innumerable infinitesimal particles of structure smaller than Quantum particles of the size of the hypothetical superstring of 10^{-33} cm value of Plank constant) or even possible further division. One finally attains the status of Emptiness, which is imperceptible to CS. The process is analogous to the splitting of atoms in the production mechanism of an atomic bomb. As a result, Emptiness is empowered with tremendous energy. Along with the Creation of energy, Omniscience is also created according to the rule of Duality,_

Therefore, Form and Emptiness are identical in nature. Due to the veil of Ignorance of Humans at his time, Buddha bypassed the explanation of the chain reaction in the formation from Emptiness to subatomic particles to atoms and molecules.

.... *Look at the element of earth which ranges in size from the great earth to a tiny speck of dust. Split this speck, which is near to nothing, and reduce it to the finest mote on the extreme border of Form. Then split it again and it becomes the Void.*

Buddha continues explaining that if the splitting keeps going on infinitely, to reduce to nothing (imperceptible to five sensory organs), the Form becomes the Void. As a result, in **the Tathàgata store (Buddhahood) both Form and (its opposite) the Void arise from self-nature and are identical to each other**

---

*.... Look at the element of earth which ranges in size from the great earth to a tiny speck of dust. Split this speck which is near to nothing and reduce it to the finest mote on the extreme border of form. Then split it again and it becomes the void. Ananda, if this mote can be reduced to nothing, you should know that form comes from the void. You now ask about material changes which you attribute to the mixing and uniting (of the four elements). Take, for instance, this mote which is nearest to the void; how much voidness should be mixed and united to produce it? But it is absurd to suppose that this can be done by uniting motes. Since a mote can be split and reduced to Emptiness, how many (particles of) forms should be fused together to create the void? The union of form (with form) produces form but not voidness, and the union of the void (with the void) produces voidness but not form. Form can be split up but how can the void unite (with form)? . You **do not know that in the Tathàgata store both form and (its opposite) the void arises from self-nature and are identical with each other,** and that the element of earth is fundamentally pure and clean, embraces all in the Dharma realm and manifests because the Minds of living beings know and distinguish (between things) in accordance with the laws of Karma. Ignorant wordlings wrongly attribute this to cause, condition and the state of the self as such, because **their Consciousnesses differentiate and discriminate without their knowing that the language they use has no real meaning** .*

You do not realize that in the Tathàgata store both fire and (its opposite) the void arises from the self-nature and are identical with each other, and that the element of fire is fundamentally pure and clean, embraces all in the Dharmarealm and manifests because the Minds of living beings know and distinguish (between things). ânanda, you should know that fire is produced wherever a man holds a mirror (in the sun), and that if mirrors are held up throughout the Dharma-realm, fire will spring up everywhere in accordance with the laws of Karma and not in a given place and direction. Ignorant worldlings wrongly attribute this to cause, condition and the state of the self as such without realizing that it is because their Consciousnesses differentiate and discriminate and that the language they use has no real meaning.

> *... Magicians obtain water to mix with their medicines by exposing a crystal ball to the full moon. Does this water come from the ball, the void or the moon?....*
> Of interest, Buddha pointed out that *element of earth is fundamentally pure and clean, embraces all in the Dharma realm and manifests (because form and void are identical) but their Consciousnesses (veil of ignorance) differentiates and discriminates without their knowing that the language they use has no real meaning. Similarly fire and (its opposite) the void arise from the self-nature and are identical.*

In summary, splitting an earth piece generates specks of imperceptible dust, equivalent to the Void/ Emptiness. Therefore, Form and Emptiness are identical in Boddhahood but nonidentical for the human discriminative Mind.

For the generation of the fire (or water), the same mechanism is applied: Fire (or water) are identical. Fire ultimately comes from the Void not from the Sun.

In the Heart Sutra, Buddha said to Sariputa that Matter is just immaterial, the immaterial is just matter (Form is Emptiness and the Emptiness per se is form, or The world is not different from Emptiness and Emptiness is not different from the world).

EMPTINESS □ THE FORM
EMPINESS □ THE FORM

Nevertheless, the two above paths of the transformation are not identical. *This is due to the asymmetry or the Duality of the world like Yin and Yang.* For example, the chicken is killed to be made into the meat. But assembling chicken meat can not make the chicken. The problem is in the process of division of chichen, the Soul (with its base, the Original Omniscience) is lost. To recreate the chicken, Omniscience (The Creator) must be added to the process.

Of interest, in this concept of Form and Emptiness that is identical in nature, Apanishads called Fullness instead of Emptiness: *"From Fullness, fullness come, when fullness is taken from fullness, fullness still remains."*

EM is UO/OM/Almighty Miracle/Mind/Spirit: God/Creator):
Not perceptible to the five senses especially
but to the CS and especially to the awareness . The Dark Force and gravity are also closely related ti EM.

In Buddha's example of splitting visible material, energy is created in the process of splitting a material. The phenomenon is similar to the process of splitting atomic particles into quantum particles to create an atomic bomb. Moreover, according to the Duality Principle, when creating energy, it also creates Mind. Energy is related to form, as evidenced in Einstein equation of $E=mc^2$, the Mind represents the invisible part of the split components.

Furthermore, when dividing objects into quantum particles and smaller ones, in addition to the generation of the Mind, The Mind is composed of components that are difficult to recognize and conceive:

- Artichectural concept of the material
- Laws/rules for the combination or interconnection of particles. This represents the part of UO that connects. Thus, UO naturally exists in the composition of matter or EM.

EN is the UO knowing everything in the Multiverse. It can be understood by saying: "Big is inside and small is not outside". Standing on the rational or scientific concept, UO is the set of all the laws of the universe:

- The Three Nature of the EM (the Inner Order of Bohm /Implicate Order):

Self-Existence, Permanece, and Oneness.

- The other attributes (Eight Negation of the Middle School):

Neither birth Nor death

Neither end Nor continuity

Neither identity Nor Difference

Neither coming Nor going

Addition attributes

Hypersymmetricity, Uniformity, Asymmetric in the Dualistic, the Law of the Ocean, the Power of Archimedes, determined to Euclid, Newton's Law of Attraction, Einstein's Relative Theory, Gödel's Incomplete Theory, Bohr's and Heisenberg's Concept of the Plural, M theory, 11 dimension theory (10 dimensions, time, possibilities, probability...) and spacetime). The other part is Power.

In summary, EM is manifested into Power, and UO is composed of Three-Self-Natures, Eight Negations, and all attributes, including all laws. EM manifestation is equivalent to Creator, God, Boudhahood, and Spirit. The EM manifestation is initiated by an activity commonly known in Buddhism as Thought or in the Old Testament as Spirit movement (God's active force) to and fro over the surface of water (darkness and waste)

Principle of Default Mode of Perfection and Almighty Power. EM is neither good nor bad, neither right nor wrong, neither omniscient nor ignorant. But when there is an initiation for change, polarization occurs (bipolarity of the Yand/Positivity and Yin/Negativity, the Yang is predominant). Thus, according to this principle of Default Mode, Perfection and Almighty power are the common expressions and views of all creatures.

B. CONTROVERSIAL INTERPRETATIONS OF BUDDHA'S TEACHINGS REGARDING THE EMPTINESS.

It is necessary to review Buddhism's spread, division into different branches and development after Buddha entered Nirvana at each council meeting (at least four),. It is also essential to understand that Buddha's teachings varied according to various levels of knowledge of human beings, ranging from practical and straightforward to conceptual and complex for beings beyond the learning stage like Arahats or Bodhisatsavas (skt: Asaika, vn: vô học).

Since the second council, there has been a subdivision of the Theravada and Mahayana groups into subgroups. Among the Theravada group, the Mūlasarvāstivāda subgroup (Nhất thiết Hữu bộ) is the most distinct by its concept of the actual existence of all Dharmas explicitly the true existence of the worldly life and existence of the Past, Present, and Future times with the Creation of Abhidharma jnànaprasthàna sàstra

These views are opposed by the Mahayana groups and the Yochara division, including Asvaghoṣa/ vn: Mã Minh 80 –

150 CE, as a <u>Mahayana</u> patriarch, Nāgārjuna/ vn: Long thụ 150–250, 14th Indian Mahayana Buddhism Patrirarch, attaining spiritual power to retrieve the Avatamsaka/ Flower sutra from the Dragon palace of the Dragon Kings, at the bottom of the ocean, Asanga/ vn: Vô Trước 300-377, attaining Arahatship from Hinayna school and being further advanced in enlightenment with Maitreya in Tusita Heaven (the Delightful Realm, the abode of Bodhisattvas in their last existence before attaining Buddhahood) and his young half-brother Vasubandhu/ vn:Thế Thân/ Duy Thức Tông/ Vijñānavādin 316-396, the 21th of Indian Mahayana Buddhism Patriarch. Avatamsaka is the most profound sutra with the concept of innumerable things and phenomena as the oneness of the Multiverse. The above Sutra and other sutras from the Mahayana school, like Flower Adornment, Diamond, Prajñāpāramitā Hṛdaya Sūtra, and Sutra/ Heart sutra only consider Emptiness the real entity. All phenomena, dharmas, are born from Emptiness and represent the secondary phenomena in the Multiverse of Duality. Time (Past, Present, and Future) and space are illusional and unreal. It is worth noting the concept of epistemology (study of the origin of CS) of Chandrakirty, a Buddhist philosopher with Indian and Tibetan influence. He said, "Whatever has causal powers (*arthakriyāsamartha*), that exists (*paramārthasat*)". *Therefore, some entities are real*. The real is only the momentarily existing particulars (*svalakṣaṇa*), and any universal (*sāmānyalakṣaṇa*) is unreal and fiction. Furthermore, for Chandrakirty, *Emptiness in Buddhism is not knowing the object. Therefore, all Mind and mental factors (Omniscience) have ceased* in Emptiness.

In common thinking and in Taoism, "*Tao is to lower the high and raise the low, to take from those who have too much and give to those who do not have enough*". Therefore, there is no emptiness per se in this Universe, knowing that the Dark Matter and/ or (?) Dark Force are imperceptible to five sensory organs, likely present in the Emptiness.

Furthermore, separating the form into tiny parts of the Quantum level and beyond the Quantum level is laborious and energy-consuming. This process is comparable to splitting materials, like uranium nuclei, into subatomic particles (quarks) in the process of creating atomic bombs with the generation of enormous energy (strong force). This means that Emptiness contains a tremendous amount of energy. Since Emptiness is boundless, its energy is inexhaustible.

When considering the energy, it is reasonable to consider the Ultimate Omniscience (UO), which is the source of Consciousness (understanding), and Awareness, which is broad but superficial in details.

The "Way" also represents Emptiness or Tao, as Lao Tsu said:
The Tao that can be told is not the eternal Tao.
The name that can be named is not the eternal name.
The nameless is the beginning of Heaven and Earth.
The name is the mother of the ten thousand things.

C, THE WORLD, AS A FALSE PERCEPTION/ PROJECTION)
Bodhisatva Nagarjuna

further developed into the philosophy of the Middle Way/ Mūla-Madhyamaka-kārikā), between the Emptiness Doctrine (Sunnyavada) and the Doctrine from the Theravada Group. Vaibhasika and Sautrantika Group of the Theravada Group accept the existence of the reality of Dharma and the world. The difference between these two groups is the concept of timing. For the Vaisahasika, the world exists in four phases: Birth, Development, Maintenance, and Death. For the Sautrantika, there is only the present, without the past or future).

In summary, the difference between Mahayana and Hinayana resides in the standpoint of view: With the perspective of view of Emptiness, Dharma and the Form are created and, therefore, perishable. If the standpoint is just after the Creation of the Sautrantika Group (vn: Kinh Lượng Bộ),, there is no concept of time, but Form and Dharma are just created. For the Vaibhasika (vn: Nhất Thiết Hữu Bộ), the standpoint of view is later in the Creation. As a result. For Hinduism perspective, the concept is still limited within the three worlds of reincarnation/Trailokya, the concept of

Emptiness, no time-space and Egolessness does not pose this kind of controversy.

D. WHY, IN CHRISTIANITY OR BUDDHISM, IS THERE NO MENTION OF THE TREMENDOUS ENERGY AND TEMPERATURE RELEASED AT THE CREATION?

For the physicist, BB begins with a tremendous burst of energy. It is a necessary condition to create the Universe. The force expands the Universe, and the heat makes everything in Space, so when it cools, it shrinks into particles, atoms, and celestial bodies.

In the scriptures of Christianity or Buddhism, it is often referred to the intention of God or the False thought, but not to the tremendous energy or terrible temperature that explodes from EM.

Looking back at Creation, we see that the three primary forces are the electromagnetic and weak and strong forces belonging to the visible world. The Dark Forces cannot be proven by science or demonstrated by CS belonging to the MW. The gravitational forces or gravity are intermediaries between PW and MW because they relate to visible matter and DM. Still, science has not proven that some types of elementary particles carry this force. Dark Force and Dark Matter account for 95% of the Universe. The PW accounts for the remaining 5% of the Universe. So, the phenomena of high temperatures and the Universe's expansion that are seen as belonging to the PW are insignificant.

Furthermore, the Dark Force is the most significant force that generates the Creation. Because the human senses do not perceive this force, the explosion conceived by the physicists is more of an illusion than truth; in other words, man did not perceive the blast. The explosion, as it is, only showed 5% of events in the world.

E. FALSE THOUGHT FROM THE EMPTINESS VERSUS BIG BANG SINGULARITY.

As mentioned above, in the Creation of the Universe, Emptiness was discussed by philosophers like Spinoza as Substance, Lao Tsu as Fuzzy Space and Void, in the Old Testament as Formlessness,

Void / nothingness, Darkness, Watery Deep, and in Islam as nothingness "creatio ex nihilo".

This concept of Emptiness as the origin of the Creation was later highlighted by (Bodhisattsava) Asvaghosa (80 – c. 150 CE, vn: Ma Minh), considered the first Patriarch who developed this concept of Mahayana deviated from the Hinayana. This concept consists of Emptiness as the ultimate origin of the Creation (Tathata with Sunyada). Tathata with Emptiness as Creator is considered as the ontological concept. The Creation and all following attributes constitute the phenomena. Because phenomenon is a secondary attribute without self-nature/noumenon (Nihilism with Negativity and Relativity. It appears that the concept is similar to Hinduism/ Upanishads concept of Fullness. However, the concept of Emptiness is original from Buddha revelation and distinct frm that of Brahmaism, part of Hinduism

F. CHARACTERISTICS OF EM
Bodhisatva Nagarjuna

characterized Emptiness with:
Three self-natures:
As a result of all the above discussions on Emptiness, it can be described as follows:

a) Three self natures, noumental characteristics, Prakriti or or Svabhava (skt))
    i. Self-existence,
    ii. Oneness
    iii. Selfness, Real Egoism, Real Ownership

b) Eight negativities:
    i,ii. No birth, no death
    iii,iv. No going No coming (*Thus come Thus go*)
    v,vi. No difference No similarity (No discrimination).

Exemplified by the Fractal phenomenon that implies similarities in geometry on a large and small scale (Fig 1.7)

The useful application is the discovery of the structure of atoms similar to that of the solar system by Niels Bohr

    vii,viii. No continuity No discontinuity: everywhere is different (because of different locations), but identical.

Accounting for Non-locality and Entanglement of Quantum phenomenon

c) Other aributes are:
- No time and space, such asn at the beginning of the Big Bang/Genesis or False thought, time and space are zero as expressed by Einstein's equation.

$Ds^2 = dx^2 + dy^2 + dz^2 - dt^2$ with $s=0$ $t=0$ and $x,y,z=0$

After the Creation, $t>0$ and $s>0$, therefore $x,y,z>0$

- Possession of unlimited power despite the consummation of the power, such as in the case of the Big Bang, the expansion keeps accelerating with the speed of expansion exceeding that of the light. No heat, No coldness
- Omniscience. The knowledge is, as the thing is, independent of the subject. In addition to the Omniscience, other properties are:
    - Construction, Creation
    - Maintenance
    - Destruction
    - Ingenuity, skill, cleverness.
- Four immeasurable Minds associated with selflessness (Immeasurable love -skt: Metta, Immeasurable kindness— Boundless compassion/ skt: Karuna in sharing sufferings, Immeasurable sharing joy/ skt: Mudita — Immeasurable detachment/ Perfect equanimity/ skt Upeksha.
- **The two most essential characteristics** often ignored in Buddhist discourse are:
    - the invisibility of EM. As a result, the activity in EM become "supernatural/metaphysical and magical" likely because elementary particles are beyond Quantum in nature, undetectable by the five senses.
    - supraluminal speed or communication

Quantumm particle entanglement and non-locality) when referring to Quantum particles that are considered close to EM, there is intercommunication with each other as in EM). Similarly, in the macro world, when the Minds of two people are directed towards the same problem, they should feel the same. It is also the method of divination of the Orient when the guesser and the watchers share a problem together, and their Minds harmoniously connect together.)

Similarly, when it comes to Photons, Photons can be recognized in more than two forms of: waves and particles. When waves are seen, light with Photons is present, and vice versa. This phenomenon is expressed as Tunelling mechanism: diaphragm may block the Photon, but the waveform can pass through a little bit.. The effect is that there is light on the other side of the membrane.

For further clarification of features of Emptiness, additional features:
- **No Time and No Space means: Thus come-Thus gone or Thusness/ Thathagata. As a result, the speed is *supraluminal*.**
- **The Emptiness is imperceptible, therefore permanent and real, not perishable. Something perceptible is impermanent (because it is perishable), and is, therefore, not real, non-existent, and illusional.**

Emptiness shares imperceptibility with illusion. However, the illusion is non-existent, created and ceases.
(In Diamond Sutra, paragraph 26, Buddha said: If one sees me in forms, If one seeks me in sounds, He practices a deviant way, and cannot see the Tathàgata).
- Ingenuity, Unlimited power, Ultimate Mind. And,
- Unthinkable miracles in the material, non-material worlds,

In terms of Physics, Emptiness has the lowest Entropy=zero. (according to the second thermodynamic law, Entropy measures the degree of intrinsic disorder or perturbation of a system. As a result, Entropy (degree of disturbance) is inversely proportional to the energetic efficacy of the system)

In other words, Emptiness is symmetrical and homogenous; therefore it is associated with a high level of energy but the lowest level of stability. As a result, spontaneous False thought may occur at times, resulting in symmetry breaking.

Testament or Buddhist sutras did not describe the terrible temperature at about one billionth of a second after the Big Bang. Know that the Buddha said so before when he said that the sermon was just as holding a leaf in his hand that the Buddha's knowledge was as much as the leaves in the woods and the Buddha's words were like what it is, and is non-illusional.

It is necessary to remind the EM that is referred to as an Abyss in the Old Testament, the Fuzziness in Taoism, and the Fullness in Hinduism.

As a result, Emptiness in Buddhism always contains something in order but is not accessible to Consciousness or the five sensory organs. For this state of order, the beginning of the Genesis, Creation, or the Big Bang is triggered by the movement of the spirit of God, / the Big Bang from a point with an accumulation of tremendous energy /or from the False thought in Buddhism. The Creation develops secondary to the loss of the equilibrium/order.

In Buddha's address to Ananda in the meeting of 1250 Arahats were registered in the Surangama sutra,
The sermon mentioned in paragraph 1), page 70 above, denotes that the Void/ Emptiness conceived in Buddha's teachings is a homogeneous, still, non-discriminative, and boundless state. As a result, a False thought eventually arises at "any point" in this state (of no space!) and instantly involves every area of the Void/ Emptiness. Since the energy in the Void is unimaginable, the False thought is enough to create the heat necessary for the fusion reaction to form particles. This energy is also responsible for expanding the space created after the Big Bang, along with the Creation of time. The arising of the False thought from the Emptiness accounts for the fact that the Cosmic Microwave Background Radiation came in from all directions of the Universe as opposed to the Big Bang Singularity as thought initially.

The above phenomenon shows that the event or object has many properties of the vacuum, there are many properties connected throughout, without distinction. This gives the feeling of having information transmitted at the speed of supraluminal communication.

> The idea is similar to that of David Bohm, that the object is the whole (wholeness) consisting of an implicate order and an explicate order forming a hologram in which each part of the hologram represents the whole of the larger part. And that's also the concept of fractal

Waves and particles do not show up together, because of the problem of observing when one pays attention, that is, using knowledge to see particles, one only see waves because knowledge obscures particles that are too small, so the Consciousness will generate waves, and vice versa (please see page 95)

The EM is not associated with Form. Because there is no Form, the the entity lasts forever. Therefore, the Buddha said, "Whoever seeks me by image or sound is evil." **Emptiness must be differentiated** from Illusion That is created and is associated with birth and death

d. Morphic Field

As a phenomenon studied by Rupert Sheldrake of the University of Cambridge UK for over 30 years, Sheldrake hypothesizes that there is a type of memory in all species that increases this type of memory to become a habit in future generations. Sheldrake called it the Morphic Resonance reaction. Examples are phenomena seen in the reproduction of creatures, including microbes, plants, animals, and humans, in the development mechanisms from embryology to social activities.

- Fractal phenomena (homogeneous mathematical engineering) like snowflakes, how branches of trees, and leaves of trees are analog, and hands and feet are analog.
- Fruit Flies' eggs exposed to diethyl ethyl change the two-winged flies into four-winged flies in a few cases. If the experiment is repeated many times, the ongoing variation occurs more and more frequently.

- IQ tests are getting higher, not because humans are smarter but because of morphic resonance.
- The dog is aware that its owner is coming home at different times.
- When one thinks of a friend, one usually gets the phone at a later time.
- Sheldrake goes even further, arguing that the feeling of seeing beyond the boundaries can be passed on to the person who is seen, causing the person to feel looked on.

The phenomenon is repeated from past to future, occurring in all fields from chemistry, physics (small fleck of ice will accelerate the ince formatin of water at zero degree), biology, and psychology (crying or laughing is contagious), making the researcher surprised, baffling, and even snooky. The phenomenon is similar to the implicate order proposed by David Bohm, Quantum Entanglement in Quantum Mechanics. All of this can be simplified in the "Neither homogenous Nor Heterogenous" phenomenon of Emptiness/EM: each place is different in place but has the same nature in the Near EM realm. The phenomenon is the entire connection of each point in a n Near EM environment. Similarly, the movement speed in this environment is supraluminal, instantaneous information. If we think the phenomenon is related to memory, we cannot explain the transmission faster than light. Another explanation for this change is epigenetic change. In the case of a dog's Telepathy, it cannot be explained with epigenetics because there are no more than two generations of Dogs. Moreover, the mechanism of Morphic Resonance is also fiercely criticized as pseudoscience for science-based mechanisms that do not reflect physical law. In summary, the morphological field can be simply regarded as a manifestation of a main characteristic of Emptiness/EM, which is "neither homogeneous nor heterogeneous. In the EM or Near EM realm, all points are interconnected with supraluminal speed, as Quantum particles show Quantum entanglement. The further distant from EM, the less noticeable Morphic Fields are.

G. PARAMITA and SELFLESSNESS

Paramita means the other shore of the river, the Nirvana, as compared to this shore of Birth and Death.
In Lankavatara Buddha distinguished three types:
- Paramitas of the supreme ones of Bodhisattva
- Paramitas for Sravakas and PratyekaBuddhas relating to the future
  - Paramitas for people, in general, relating to this world

In all cases, Paramita represents the state of Selflessness, commonly used in the Four Immeasurable Minds (Love, Compassion, Inner Joy, and Detachment). The principle is that human beings are children of the Creator, do not own anything in this world, and do not have free will.
All materials and love given away belong to the Creator. Happiness only results from the fulfillment of the duty instructed by the Creator.

H. Only God is the footer of love. Saint Augustine (Aurelius Augustinus Hipponensis) the theologian born in 354 in Algeria initiated the name of the original sin. This makes the synonym of God close to EM/Budhahood. However, the concept of Christianity in the personalization of God in in Form, while Buddhism believes that Buddhood belongs to the EM Realm.
The difference is easy to understand because the Buddhahood/God is in the Realm of Primordial Duality that possesses both features of Duality and EM.

Another fundamental dynamic similarity is the expression of the Trinity (God, Jesus, and the Spirit) in Christianity and the (trikāya) (*dharmakāya/Dharma body*, *saṃbhogakāya/Bliss body* and *nirmāṇakāya*)/Emanational Body in Buddhism.

Aerial legs are powerful and powerful.
 (Buddha/Miracle/Mind/Spirit:God/Creator):
It is not felt by the ear, but the wisest is the feeling.
received, so Dark Force and Weight also belong to the Airfoot.

Again, in the process of splitting in the example of splitting from the visible body to the Buddha's Airfoot, energy will be created.

The phenomenon is similar to splitting atomic particles into quantum particles to create an atomic bomb. Moreover, according to the Secondary Principle, when creating energy, it also creates Mind. That's the good mind.

When dividing objects into quantum particles and smaller ones: in addition to the production of nuts, there are two components that are difficult to recognize and conceive:
• Strength
• Mechanism—rules and kindness combine particles. This is the part of THBN that connects the particles. Thus THBN is naturally present in the composition of matter or CK due to no vision.

THBN is the Supreme Mind, knowing everything in the Multiverse. It can be expressed by saying: The big is inside and the small is not outside. Standing on the rational or scientific concept, THBN is the set of all the laws of the universe: CK's Three Self, the Infinite Bowl of Longevity, Bohm's Inner Order (Implicate Order), Supersymmetry in Uniformity, Invincibility in Childhood, Ocean Law, Archimede's Power, Destination to Euclid, Newton's Law of Attraction, Einstein's Theory of Relativity, Godel's Incomplete Theory, Bohr and Heisenberg's Summary Concept, M theory, 11 dimension theory (10 dimensions, time, possibilities, probability...) and spacetime). The synthesis of the appropriate rules of rule is THBN, which is the component of the superior crab. The other part is power.

V. UNDERSTANDING OF THE IGNORANCE and THREE SEALS OF DHARMA, Four Kinds of Mindfulness Eightfold Path

The EM is indestructible, equal, and super-symmetric. Although it is often permanent, it is easy to lose balance (see Figure F7). So when there is a shift that can be right Mindfulness, EM retains the same characteristics as EM, but there is time and space like Heaven/Nirvana. In case of false Mindfulness/False thought, EM is destroyed and is replaced with this PW. So, the Creation is composed of the Nirvana and this PW. Following the

Creation, the Universe is born to be destroyed and has no true selfness.

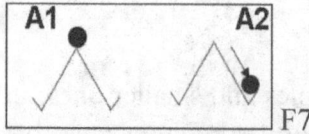
F7

In the PW, Selflessness, Impermanence, and Suffrance are characteristically essential in Buddhist dharmas along with 37 factors of enlightenment (Four Right Efforts, Four Sufficiences, Four Kinds of Mindfulness, The Five Faculties, The Five Powers, Seven Bodhi Shares, Noble Eightfold Path: right view, right aspiration, right speech, right action, right livelihood, right effort, right Mindfulness, right concentration.). Failure to recognize the three Seal Dharmas is due to ignorance, which will lead to an inversion view of the world.

In life, the common pathway of recognition of the three Dharmas is the observation of the earthly phenomena and using the induction method. This method may be associated with the potential for error. The other method of recognition of the three Seals of Dharma are:

   a) **Buddha recommends the technique of Four Kinds of Mindfulness.**

*Contemplation of the body, realization of the serenity or impurity of the body.

* Contemplation of Feeling, realization of the evils of sensations or pleasant feelings, no matter whether they are painful, joyous, or indifferent sensations

* Contemplation of the Mind, the evils or the virtue of the thought and Mind, the realization of the different states of Mind (Greed, Anger and Ignorance or Immeasurable Mind of virtue)

* Contemplation of Dharmas or the origination of the Mind, realization formation of the Mind

   b) **Ontological Method .**

following the Universe's Creation, the Creator is the oneness who is the father of all living Beings and Owner of all other physical and metaphysical entities. Human beings are given the conditions for living, working/ creating, and entertainment commensurable to their needs. The extra givings belong to the Creator and are available to living sentients to share with the others. The body, the feeling, the Mind, and Nature are selfless, owned by the Creator.

Thoughtful understanding and realization of this principle are almost equivalent to the Mindful contemplation in the above four areas.

As a result, the realization of Selflessness and detachment from erroneous ownership is the key to Mindful contemplation to eradicate the bad Mind, as told by Buddha to Ananda and Rahula in Nikaya Sutra 61

In PW, Grief is the hallmark of all creatures. Buddha said that when humans hadn't realized that life was suffering, man was still wandering in six realms if reincarnation (Deva, Asura, Man, Animal, Satan, Hell). The Four Noble Truths are to remember that life is the ocean of sorrow, suffering is caused by the three poisons (Greed Anger, and Ignorance), liberation from suffering is possible and is the path of cultivation with the 37 factors of enlightenment, the most important of which is the Eightfold Path of Virtue: Right Effort, Thought, Language, Profession, Memory, Thinking, View, and Meditation.

VI. The Darwin Theory G. DARWINISM.
1. The theory.
The book of Darwin (Charles Darwin 1809- 1882) entitled "On the Origin of Species," published in 1859, is about the origin of the earthly life. In his book, Darwin's opinion contradicts the previous common opinions that favor life incidentally develops. According to scientific theory, the epistemological (knowledge–related) development of life is neither accidental nor theological. The species develop in the direction of conforming/ adapting to the environment. *Those with an appropriately high capability of adaptation will prevail over those with a low potential for adaptation.* With evolution lasting for billions of years, the adaptation and the differentiation resulting in the selection mechanism render different species different from each other.

Recent understanding of the epigenetic phenomenon (related to the expression of genes without mutation of the gene) has added an important mechanism of adaptation by bypassing gene mutation.

In this mechanism, alterations of histone, type of protein supporting chromosomes, and genes can modify the expression of the genes. This type of adaptation, equivalent to learning, can pass from parent to children and shorten the time course of evolution from millions of years to months/ and years, from many generations to parents-children's generations. Children of parents with poor nutrition tend to develop diabetes mellitus.

2. Social Darwinism.
On a larger scale, Darwinism can apply to societies or countries. In society, ethnic groups with a high potential for adaptation tend to be more prosperous than other groups.
Comments: Darwinism had received a welcome from the scientific community at the time. Many of his findings still prevail today. However, the role of chance/ contingency and natural selection is difficult for further scientific confirmation than what he had proved. The problem of chance and contingency in the Creation of human beings is challenging to prove or disprove. Scholastic phenomenon, as seen in the case of a handful of sand containing granules of sand of different sizes. The granules are independent of one another, but they still represent a continuum of change. This phenomenon purely occurs by chance, not by selection.

Furthermore, in Darwinism, it seems that Darwin tried to distance himself from Genesis/ the Creation of the Universe, probably the domain of religion at his time.

3. Origin of life.
In the 1950s, Urey, a Nobel Prize Laureate in Physics and Chemistry, and Miller, a young Ph.D. collaborator, had successfully made organic compounds from mineral materials. They synthesized amino acids in test tubes containing water (H_2O), methane (CH_4), ammonia (NH_3), hydrogen (H_2), and an electric arc (the latter simulating hypothesized lightning). The experiment simulated the condition of the primitive early Earth

and supported the hypothesis of <u>Alexander Oparin</u>. In his hypothesis, Oparin suggested that complex organic compounds are synthesized due to favorable conditions, a gradual evolution from inorganic to organic compounds under an oxygen-poor atmosphere.

Haldane in the USA also predicted that organic compounds of intermediate molecular weight represent the transitional form between mineral compounds and viruses. (Haldne 2003).

The virus was first discovered in 1917.
These findings can formulate the pathway of the evolution of inorganic to organic compounds. Another significant step is the discovery of ribosomes, microscopic granules of RNA playing the intermediate step in the synthesis of protein from DNA. Again, in the
Creation of the Universe, the question remains whether DNA or protein is the original precursor, similar to the question of egg and chicken.

4. The Cell Theory.
According to Rudolf Virchow and Louis Pasteur, life only starts from another life. This leads to the problem of searching for a life that can originally start. *Scientists look for life in other parts of the Universe to unlock the mystery or even for life to emigrate to our planet.* For all living organisms, the cells are relatively uniformly composed of:
i. Cell membrane forming the boundaries of individual cells.
ii. Cytoplasm containing organelles for reproduction, development, and basic metabolism, and
iii. Coils of DNA for reproduction and synthesis of proteins.

5. Gap in the evolution.
According to Darwinism, humans, Chimpanzees, and Bonobos share a common "ancestor" (regarding the physical similarities), that is, Hominini based on DNA and gene studies. Despite the close relationship between the physical components, the metaphysical part is completely different. Furthermore, there is a remarkable gap in the mental status between chimpanzees and

humans, not only in emotion, thinking, and creativity but, importantly, in morality.

12millions   millions of   millions of years (in Africa)
⇩   ⇩   ⇩
Great Apes→ Homonids→Homoninae →Gorillas
↘   ↘ Hominini →Chimpanzee + Bonobo
Orangutans   ↘ Homo Sapiens
GAP BETWEEN HUMAN-ANIMAL ⇧ is **MORALITY**

6. The first Man and Woman (suggestive of Adam and Eva in the Paradise in The Old Testament are doubtful) ?78
Mitochondrial DNA (mtDNA) in men and women (mitochondria are considered the powerhouse of the cell) is of maternal origin since, at fertilization, only the spermatozoa's nucleus enters the ova. Analysis of mtDNA showed that all human mtDNA share the same mtDNA of the same ancestor woman (hence named mtDNA Eva) living in Africa. Analysis of chromosome Y containing gene SRY activated in men also demonstrated that all chromosome Y share the same Y chromosome Y of the ancestor man.

Since 1985, the above questions have been discussed and studied at larger scales.
The name Eve does not represent the historic name but is symbolic. It is questionable that Eve is not the only woman of her time. Adam may live in a time before or even after Eve. Furthermore, mt DNA can be found in chimpanzees, bonobos, and even in animals of lower scale in phylogenetic evolution.

Humans emigrated from Eastern Africa to Europe, Asia, and North America when the continent was still connected to Asia.
The above pathway of evolution and development can be found in the following Sermon in Nikaya Sutra, chapter 27/ *Aggañña Sutta: On Knowledge of Beginnings (Long Discourses) (page 52)*:
Buddha 's teachings are summarized as follows:
.... And sooner or later, after a very long period of time, savory earth spread itself over the waters where those beings were. It looked just like the skin that forms itself over hot milk as it cools... 12.

'Then some being tasted the savory earth on its finger. ... **So they set to with their hands, breaking off pieces of the stuff in order to eat it. ... The result of this was that their self-luminance disappeared**.
As a result, **the moon and the sun appeared with**, night and days, months, years and its seasons: The world re-evolved.

The faces and bodies became coarser, and a difference in looks developed among them. Some became good-looking, others ugly. **Discrimination and arrogance developed, respectively. Then, females and males developed sex organs, developed and indulged in sexual activity.** Successively, different types of crops appear

> *..And sooner or later, after a very long period of time, savoury earth spread itself over the waters where those beings were. It looked just like the skin that forms itself over hot milk as it cools. It was endowed with colour, smell and taste. It was the colour of fine ghee or butter, and it was very sweet, like pure wild honey.*
> *12. 'Then some being of a greedy nature said: "I say, what can this be?" and tasted the savoury earth on its finger. In so doing, it became taken with the flavour, and craving arose in it. Then other beings, taking their cue from that one, also tasted the stuff with their fingers. They too were taken with the flavour, and craving arose in them.* ***So they set to with their hands, breaking off pieces of the stuff in order to eat it. And [86] the result of this was that their selfluminance disappeared****. And as a result of the disappearance of their selfluminance,* ***the moon and the sun appeared****, night and day were distinguished, months and fortnights appeared, and the year and its seasons. To that extent the world re-evolved.*
> *13. 'And those beings continued for a very long time feasting on this savoury earth, feeding on it and being nourished by it. And as they did so, their bodies became coarser, and a difference in looks developed among them. Some beings became good-looking, others ugly. And the good-looking ones despised the others, saying: "We are better-looking than they are." And because they became arrogant and conceited about their looks, the savoury earth disappeared. At this they came together and lamented, crying: "Oh that flavour! Oh, that flavour!" And so nowadays when people say: "Oh that flavour!" when they get something nice, they are repeating an ancient saying without realizing it. 14. 'And then, when the savoury earth had disappeared, a fungus cropped up, in the manner of a mushroom. It was of a good colour, smell, and taste. It was the colour of fine ghee or butter, and it was very sweet, like pure wild honey. And those beings set to and ate the fungus. And this lasted for a very long time.* ***And as they continued to feed on the fungus, so their bodies became coarser still, and the difference in their looks increased still more****. And the good-looking ones despised the others ...* ***And because they became arrogant and conceited about their looks, the sweet fungus disappeared****. Next, creepers appeared, shooting up like bamboo..., and they too were very sweet, like pure wild honey. 15. 'And those* ***beings set to and fed on those creepers. And as they did so, their bodies became even coarser****, and the difference in their looks increased still more... And they* ***became still more arrogant****, and so the creepers disappeared too. At this they came together and lamented, crying: "Alas, our creeper's gone! What have we lost!" And so now today when people, on being asked why they are upset, say: "Oh, what have we lost!" they are repeating an ancient saying without realizing it. 16. 'And then, after the creepers had disappeared,* ***rice appeared in open spaces, free from powder and from husks, fragrant and clean-grained****. And what they had taken in the evening for supper had grown again and was ripe in the morning, and what they had taken in the*

> *morning for breakfast was ripe again, by evening, with no sign of reaping. And these beings set to and fed on this rice, and this lasted for a very long time. And as they did so, their bodies became coarser still, and the difference in their looks became even greater. And **the females developed female sex-organs, and the males developed male organs**. And the women became excessively preoccupied with men, and the men with women. Owing to this excessive preoccupation with each other, passion was aroused, and their bodies burnt with lust. And later, because of this **burning, they indulged in sexual activist**. But those who saw them indulging threw dust, ashes or cow-dung at them, crying: "Die, you filthy beast! How can one being do such things to another!" Just as today, in some districts, when a daughter-in-law is led out, some people throw dirt at her, some ashes, and some cow-dung, without realising that they are repeating an ancient observance. What was considered bad form in those days is now considered good form. . 'And **those beings who in those days indulged in sex were not allowed into a village or town for one or two months**. .....*

VIII. THE CREATION OF SPECIES.

As cited above, Original Awareness/ vn: Trí Huệ originates from the Original Mind/ Emptiness with the four potentials of maintenance, destruction, construction, and impeccable, ingenious, and orderly creativity. Again, these potentials are uncreated and quiescent. One can only see its effects.

In summary, following the False thought, the Emptiness creates the Form, the Metaphysical entities (and the Secondary Emptiness):

"the birth of life of all beings of the twelve (twelve is calculated as 3 [present, past and future] x 4 [east, north, west, south]) forms of living organisms despite being separated in the ten directions of space, all attached to the same root. This mythical revelation of Consciousness is at the moment (of Creation) that is equivalent to the very beginning of the dawn."

A. Parents Nurture But Do Not Create Children.

It is currently believed by evolutionary biologists, anthropologists and molecular scientists that human beings and chimpanzees share a common ancestor. For more than 150 years since Darwin published his book "On Origin of Species", the evolutionary theory has laid down cumulative evidence of the above common thinking regarding the origin of human beings. The human origin and its evolution were based on the similarity between species emphasized by Darwin and Huxley (1). Furthermore, the evolutionary and morphological features of fossil bones (skull, mandible, teeth, enamel), analysis of DNA and genome are suggestive of the occurrence of the speciation of human-chimpanzee and chimpanzee-gorilla at 6000 to 10 000 centuries ago. It is well known that the more similar species are more closely related. However, as Wallace, who supported Darwin's theory of evolution, pointed out in 1864, "Children of the same parents are not all alike". The opposite is true: look-alike people may not come from the same parents.

In this observation, the careful study of the germline in most animals shows that the germ cell line is distinct from the somatic cell groups. In early embryogenesis, the germ line cells undergo mitotic divisions at the end of the second week of post-fertilization. Each division gives rise to a germ cell and a somatic cell. After the third mitotic cell division, the germ cell undergoes meiotic cell division and differentiation into the pure germ line with further progression into ova or spermatozoa essential for species propagation. In the same period, the somatic cells derived from the germ line undergo successive mitosis, which is indispensable for the formation of body and accessory structures.
The germ cells do not originate from the somatic cells except in certain animals of low levels of phylogenetic scales, like planarians. In a developed body, germ cells are localized in the gonads (Figure 1.9).

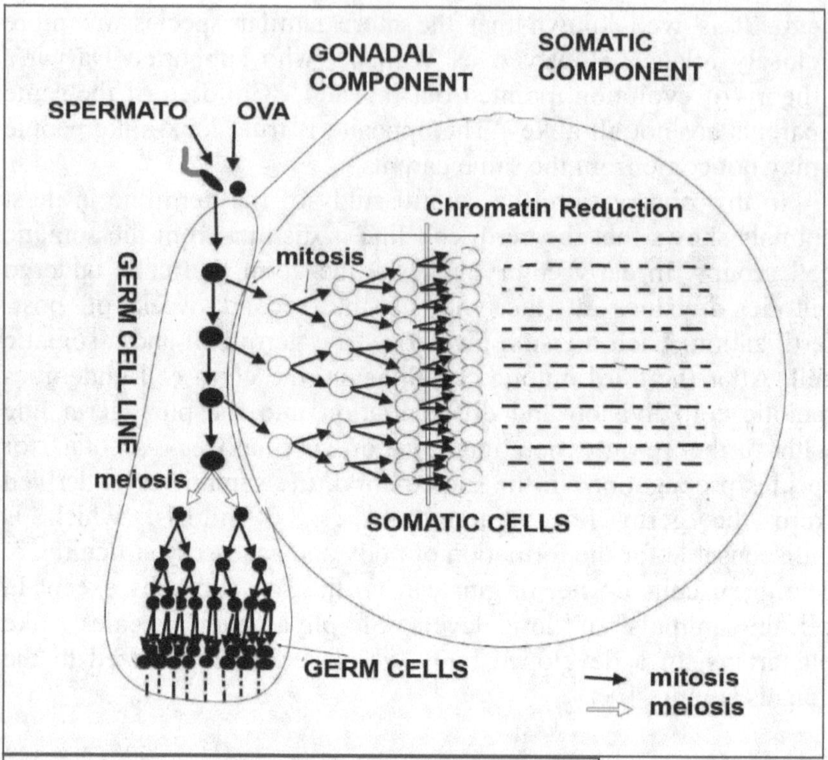

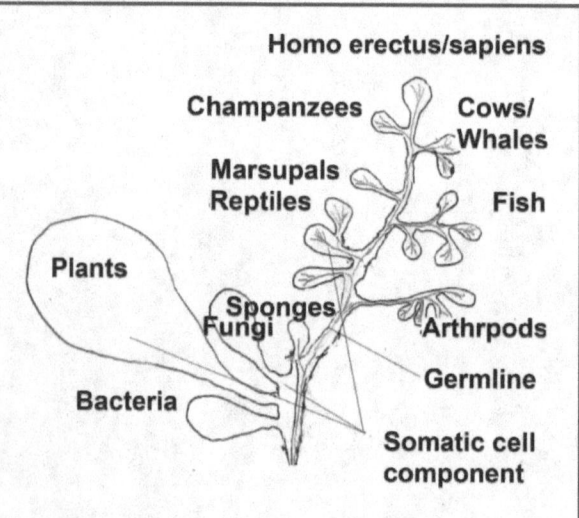

Figure 1.9   **Figure 1.10**
Showing the formation of the germ line in the gonadal component and the development of a somatic component only consisting of somatic

cells from the fertilized ova following the successive mitosis of the zygote (fertilized ova).

Figure 1.10
Proposed Phylogenetic Tree in Nature
-The tree trunk mainly consists of somatic cells for Bacteria, plants, and fungi. There is no germline coming directly from the root so-called Ultimate Creative Source
-For animals, the tree's trunk consists of two components: the somatic component, giving rise to the general configuration of the tree, and the germ line component, which originates directly from the root and in dependent on the somatic component. The somatic cells develop from the germ line cells
- All individual animals, including humans, develop from germ lines created from Creation/ Nature, regardless of the level of evolution. Germ cells are not made from the somatic cells of parents. The parents/ ancestors harbor and nurture them.
- Somatic cells and associated germ cells display the genome or DNA closest to those of their siblings, parents, and ancestors.
- The similarities in genome account for morphological changes of bone, body, and face consistent with the evolutionary morphologic relationship between different but closely related species in the evolutionary phylogeny.

B. Phylogenetic Tree Of Evolution.

The above observations do not alter Darwin's natural selection theory and do not alter the general configuration of the species' phylogenetic tree, mainly for fungi, plants, and bacteria. For these species, there is no pure germ cell lineage; the germ cells develop from the somatic cells by a special mechanism. For animals, because the germ cell line comes directly from the Ultimate Creative Source (often called Creator/ God or Buddhahood), the trunk of the phylogenetic tree consists of two parallel components: the germ cell line is distinct from the somatic cell component. The gonadal tissue that is located in the bodily cell part (Figure 2) wraps around the germ cell line.

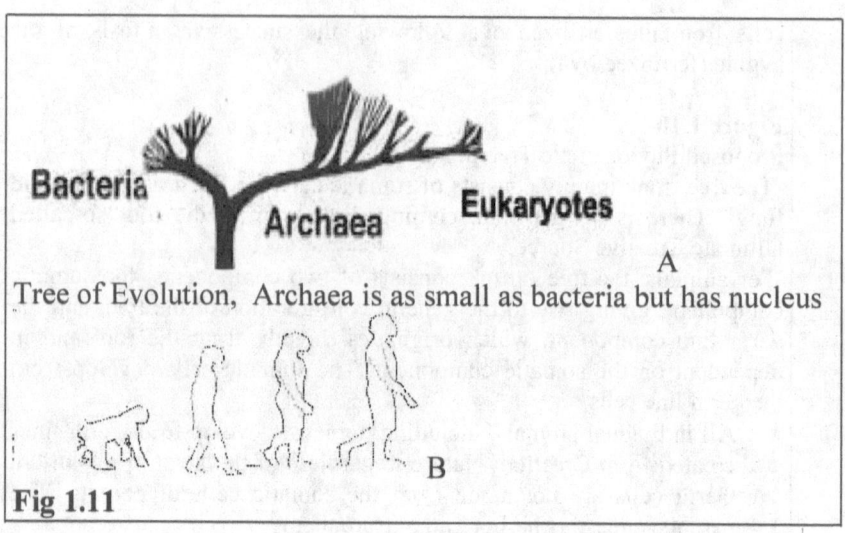

Fig 1.11 Tree of Evolution, Archaea is as small as bacteria but has nucleus

These findings may reinforce the belief in major religions (Islam, Christianity, and Buddhism) regarding the Creation of human beings directly from the Ultimate (Original) Creative Source. For Christianity and Islam, it is well known that God and Allah created Adam and Eva. In Mahayana Buddhism Surangama sutra, Buddhasaid: the birth of life of all beings of the twelve (3x4: 3= present/past future x 4= directions) forms of living organisms, although separated in the ten directions of space, all attached to the same root. This mythical revelation of Buddha's Consciousness is at the moment (of Creation) that is equivalent to the very beginning of the dawn. (J of Phylogeny Evol Biol,10:11, 2022.10.250"Parents Nurture but Do not Create Children.")

At the Meditation at the deep level, when the last veil of Ignorance is cleared out of the way for apparent Awareness, the meditator can see the birth of all species, as illustrated in this saying of Buddha at the end chapter of the Surangama sutra. As discussed in the paragraph of the veil of Ignorance , the integration of data received by the six senses constitutes a barrier from the Original Mind to get assess to the data. The data is a whole package must be split into six separate packages. The veil of Ignorance impedes humans from acknowledging the origin of species at the Creation.

In Chapter X of Surangama Sutra, Buddha reveal of the Creation:

In the Meditation, when the aggregate of formaton is cleared, the fifth aggregate of Consciousness releases the practiser from all attraction, the Mind, are clear and transparent like crystal both within and without. This is the end of the aggregate of Consciousness which enables the practiser to realize the beginning of the Creation

> *Ananda, in the cultivation of samàdhi, when the fourth aggregate of discrimination (saùskàra) comes to an end, the subtle disturbance in the state of clearness, (that is the functioning of samsaric Mind), which is the mechanism of birth and death, suddenly explodes and exposes an outlook completely different*
> *from that of the profound Karma of pudgala (, i.e. all beings subject to transmigration). This is the moment when Nirvana is about to dawn, like the cock-crow that heralds the first light of the day in the east, when the six senses are void and still and no more wander outside. Within and without there is only a profound brightness reaching the root of life of all beings of the twelve forms of birth in the ten directions of space wherein there is nothing that can be further penetrated. This contemplation of the essence of basic clinging (, i.e. the fifth aggregate of Consciousness) releases the practiser from all attraction (by old habits and new Karma) and immunizes him from further transmigration in saùsàra for he has realized the identity of Mind with its self-created externals everywhere. As the nature of Consciousness now manifests clearly, he will discover its hidden depth, This is the fifth aggregate of Consciousness which conditions the practiser's Meditation.*
> *.As the practiser is immune against external attractions and realizes the identity of Mind, and objects, the separateness arising from the six different sense organs ceases and the Mind functions uniformly with seeing and hearing in regard to a single function which is pure and clean. In this state, all the worlds in the ten directions, together with his body and Mind, are clear and transparent like crystal both within and without. This is the end of the aggregate of Consciousness which enables the practiser to leap over and beyond the kalpa of turbid life, the main cause of which is the (first) seeming shadow of his wrong thinking*

One wonders why this simple, fundamental, and very important question for human beings has been unfortunately misled. The reason is the veil of ignorance. The knowledge has been misled by science which only focuses on the epi-phenomenon of evolution. The accomplishment of technology has tremendously improved the materialistic quality of life and has rendered people to stop believing in major religious teachings. Buddha repeatedly said Buddha's teachings are not illusional!

Since human beings are so proud of themselves, with some rational thinking, one can see that if the ancestors are monkeys/chimpanzees, the ancestors of chimpanzees are lower-level animals; successively, the conclusion will be that the ancestors of human beings are insects or so... (***Wiley, EO, 2011***)

C. Conclusions.

Despite tremendous development and achievement for more than 100 years since the successful proposal of many theories with Max Planck's discovery of h constant, Albert Einstein's suggestion of light waves are quantized, Ernest Rutherford , Niels Bohr and Werner Heisenberg, Wolfgang Pauli in the design of the structure of atoms and David Bohm's concept of implicate order of the wholeness of atoms with implication in the concept of Mind and Quantum level. However, science is still limited in 5% of the Universe containing baryonic matter.

- Humans are created by the Creator. Parents or lower sentient beings only nurture children. The objection to this reality is a critical mistake due to the superficial morphologic observation with the input of the veiled Mind. Monkeys and chimpanzees do not create human beings but carry and protect human germline cells.
- The ingenious assembly and arrangement of the Creator creates the world. It is irrational that chance and accidents have to happen multiple times in Genesis to build this world as it is nowadays.
- Big Bang is still an incomplete theory for all phenomena, including logistic observation. The approach demonstrated similarities with False thought arising from Emptiness since both create a local expanding quake with acceleration to create time and space. Among the deficiencies of the

- Big Bang is the need for more ingenuity that is required at many levels of Creation, like forming minerals, trees, and sentient beings. Other phenomena like entanglement, interconnectedness,
- As a result, religion and theism are necessary and accompany worldly life.
- Buddha said in the Nikaya sutra (Long Discourse).

> 'Ananda, just as if they had taken counsel with the Thirty-Three Gods, Sunidha and Vassak Fira are building a fortress at Pzrtaligiima. I have seen with my divine eye how thousands of devas were taking up lodging there. . .(as verse 26). Ananda, as far as the Ariyan realm extends, as far as its trade extends, this will be the chief city, Pafaliputta, scattering its seeds far and [88] wide. And Pataliputta will face three perils: from fire, from water and from internal dissension.' 1.29. Then Sunidha and Vassakara called on the Lord and, having exchanged courtesies, stood to one side and said: 'May the Reverend Gotama accept a meal from us tomorrow with his order of monks!' And the Lord consented by silence

- Science is necessary for material life when humans, with the physical body, develop technology. Nevertheless, besides the physical body, the Form, the metaphysical part (Perception, Feeling, Formation, and Consciousness) is even more essential and lasts much longer. It is critical in guiding humans to everlasting happiness. Theism is necessary for the Creation of the Universe, Nature, and Species and plays an influential role in living. Religion may cause an illusional view of life with dependence on religion instead of being self-supportive and self-relying. Freud, as well as his contemporary fellows, believe that theism makes humans more dependent than to liberate them from theism.

Flower Adornment/ vn: kinh Hoa Nghiêm and Lotus/ vn: kinh Pháp Hoa are two major sutras among Buddhist sutras. Splendid, magnificent Buddha landscapes with miraculous ingenuities exceeding imagination and limitless multiple Universes. On the other hand, Surangama sutra, Buddha went into the ontologic aspect of Buddhism, laying out:
-The significance of Emptiness.
-False thought transforms the Original Mind (common to all Universes, minerals, and all sentients) into different Forms of nature, such as water, earth, mountains, and living organisms.
- The development of worldly life with inversion.

- Formation of the Consciousness by splitting the original data into six separate sources of information and the veil of ignorance, the important cause of the inversion.
 - the path of liberation from suffering.

Implication In Vegetarianism.
Vegetarianism is the practice of living depending on no-meat products, therefore abstaining from killing animals. Ovo and ovo-lacto vegetarianism allows the consumption of eggs and dairy products. Consumption of non-fertilized eggs is usually similar to milk and represents an abuse of animal welfare. However, consuming milk and dairy products is eventually indispensable for human survival and is allowable in Buddhism. Consumption of non-fertilized eggs that can carry the risk of attraction of nonphysical sentients is, therefore, not permissible.

The key point in Vegetarianism is that germline cells are strictly derived from the Creator as opposed to somatic cells in animals and vegetal cells from parents/ plants harboring vegetal buds. Somatic cells develop from germ cells, but never germ cells develop from somatic cells in animals. Therefore, animals represent the children of the Creator, while the Creator does not directly create plants, mushrooms, and bacteria. Therefore, Vegetarianism does not involve killing the children of the Creator.

Furthermore, vegetal cells can act as germ cells to create new plants, while somatic cells of Animals can not be transformed into germline cells in natural conditions. It is known that in laboratories, Somatic cells can be made to change into germline cells.

IVIII. HOW DOES THE CREATION HAPPEN? BY CHANCE OR BY GOD
Role of the Ultimate Omniscience
(vn: Trí Huệ Bát Nhã) (Fig 37,.8,9
As revealed by the Buddha, the Creation was initiated from an incidental Thought (vn: Vọng Niệm) arising from Emptiness. In some particular circumstances, Emptiness can be represented by the Implicate Order conceived by David Bohm, a theoretical

Physicist. From the original stillness, homogeneity, balance, and non-discrimintation, the Emptiness demonstrates the imperishable and unmeasurable force and the Ultimate Omniscience. Unmeasurable power accounts for all forces of the Universe, including the Dark Force causing the Universe's accelerating expansion. The Ultimate Omniescience accounts for the orderly, organized, magnificent, ingenious formation of all Forms. The Ultimate Omniescience was personalized as God in major religions. Since it was conceived by scientists (physicists and mathematicians), the Universe could not have been created as it is today by a random combination of elementary particles (Photons, bosons quarks...) in a period of 14 billion years after the Big Bang. Mathematically this Universe may require at least 1.5 times the Universe's age. As a result, the alternative mechanisms of Creation are chance or the Spiritual power of God. The chance mechanism does not seem sufficient to be responsible for multiple complicated formations of structures in nature. For example, Rudolf Virchows and Louis Pasteur believe that life can only be created from life (living cells only give birth to living cells).

IX. REASON OF CREATION. (Fig F7)

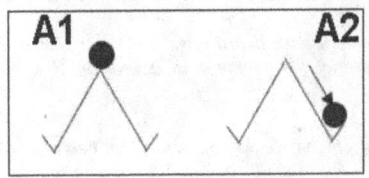

F7

In TAO or religion, contrary to physicists, the Creation from the EM is initiated not with a BB, but with a change of EM status. The reason for the difference between the concept of science based on fact and TAO or religion based on ontology will be clarified and discussed later in this b ook.
EM is uniform and super-symmetric. The Figure A1 represents symmetry and balance. The above balance is always accompanied by maintaining fragility and being prone to being unstable and turning into A2. Without any disturbance, EM is permanent and imperishable.

False thought that triggered the the Creation of the PW with the veil of ignorance. False thoughts develop by chance but are caused by mistakes after the Creation of the MW. The mistake occurs due to the misunderstanding after the Creation of the EM; Element in the new Creation could be either good or bad, but mistaken as always God, as in a can of Mr. and Mrs. Adam Eve mistakenly believed that every fruit in the Eden garden is God for eternal life. Due to the mistake considered as a sin, they stop having eternal life and develop a discriminative Mind. they do not deserve to live in the haven and are sent out of Heaven.

When there is a disturbance of EM
- *With the right Mindfulness, EM is transformed into Nirvana or Paradise because the uniformity, non-discrimination of the EM are preserved.*
- *With False Mindfulness or False thought, EM is transformed into the Creation of the realm of Passion, including the visible PW (the material world today) and non-visible, including the Hell, Realm of Hungry Ghosts, Asura, and Devas.*

The Buddha asked: Purnamaitrayaniputra, you now ask why that which is fundamentally pure and clean suddenly created mountains, rivers and the great earth. Whose Minds are set on self-enlightenment and not on Bodhisattva development, you not heard the Buddha declare that (self-) natured Bodhi is absolute and enlightened and that basic Bodhi is enlightened and absolute?

Purnamaitrayaniputra replied: Yes, World Honoured One, I have heard this.

A Probe into the Disciple's Understanding of Noumenon & Phenomenon to Reveal the Rise of Illusions

The Buddha asked: When you speak of Bodhi and Enlightenment, do you mean that because of its enlightened nature, you call it Bodhi, or because of its (basic) unenlightened nature, you (now) call it enlightened Bodhi?

The Real Missed by Cognition of the False

Purnamaitrayaniputra said: If that which is unenlightened is called Bodhi, . Self-natured Bodhi stands for Substance which is essentially absolute (i.e. free from all dualities) and is, therefore, enlightened. Basic Bodhi stands for Function Basic Ignorance

The Buddha said: You say that that which is not aware of anything is not enlightened Bodhi, but that which creates an illusory object is unenlightened and that which abstains from so doing is free from (subjective) awareness. The unenlightened is not the clean nature of Bodhi, for (self-) natured Bodhi is essentially enlightened but is mistaken for enlightened awareness. Bodhi is not (that) awareness of things for such awareness sets up objects, and the setting up of illusory objects implies an illusory subject

---

Summary: Purnamaitrayaniputra: the mechanism of developing mountains and rivers from the clear Mind.

Buddha: Original Bodhi is absolute and enlightened or not unenlightened

But natured Bodhi can be either enlightened or unenlightened but mistaken as always enlightened. The phenomenon is similar to the Sin committed by &Mrs. Adam and Eva, mistakenly believing that every fruit in the Eden Garden is good for eternal living and Omniscience, but the fruit in the center is not good, causing the discriminative Mind and shortened life.

It can be conceived that Original Bodhi (EM) creates the Dark Force, UO of the MW. When there is a mistake, Original Bodhi creates potons and the PW. Dark Matter and The Soul are intermediate between PW and MW.

In summary, EM only creates the Dark Force and UO; the visible world is created when there is a mistake in the Creation. As a result, there may be two types of worlds: visible and invisible. Dark matter, the Soul, is the intermediate matter between the above two worlds.

According to Einstein's theory of relativity, Energy and Matter are represented in the following equation applicable to the physical world.

$E = mc^2 / \sqrt{1-v^2/c^2}$ m Matter, c Ligh speed of 300.000km/sec and E Energy. *Matter is represented by the most infinitesimal by beyond Quantum particles.*

In the PW v< c, because there is no concept of metaphysical realm in science

According to Buddhist concept, EM or VOID is not empty pe se but contains beyond Quantum particles, as a result Photons is not the smallest, or massless particle, MW only represent the realm beyond the scientific measurability (i.e. DM and DF). Since beyond Quantum particle must exist, the v can be greater than c (as case of Jesus Buddha, saints Angels)

Therefore in the equation
$m = E^{\sqrt{1-v^2/c^2}} / c^2$.

When v>c,

$E = mc^2/\sqrt{1-v^2/c^2}$ is an imaginary number in the PW.
Since Black matter exists and is real, E must be virtual for this visible physical world. Since the above equation applies to the visible, virtual energy does not apply to the objects of the MW (Buddha, Bodhisatsavan celestial sentient... So, this virtual energy can be conceived as an Empirical Power symbol with Ei.
and represented by the Karmic Force, represented by the following equation

$Ei = mc^2/\sqrt{1-v^2/c^2}$ with v>c

X. EMBODIED SOUL OF THE PHYSICAL PARTS WITHOUT BRAIN

A. EMBODIED SOUL

The idea of the existence of the Embodied Soul is based on the anomaly of The Soul attached to the brain and the existence of Chi or Qi in Acupuncture and Martial arts. Embodied Soul represents the invisible part of the body according to the concept of Duality. If the Soul attached to the brain is accounted for the CS, the Embodied Soul is accounted for the strength of muscle and energy associated with acupuncture.

According to Barrett, emotional expression is not based much on customary or genetic habits but based on the Mind formed from birth. The process is similar to the Consciousness process.

B. Abdidhamma

Abdidhamma is the sermon preached by Buddha in Tsitusima Realm in the presenve of his deceased mother and other Deva. The Sermon describes emotional behavior and the mechanism that creates emotional behavior based on Consciousness, which creates emotional suffering or joy. But not to approach the mechanism of creating joy or suffering in the world.

C. The Emotion

different from the CS because emotion is the CS and is associated with endocrine, exocrine, and motor expressions. As described before, the CS in Emotion triggers the automatic center for the

secretion of hormones (steroids, epinephrine, acetylcholine), exocrine secretion (saliva, tears, the sympathetic and parasympathetic nervous system controlling lung, heart, bowel, excretory glands like tears, saliva, and muscle of face and extremities and other parts of the whole by for motor expression.
For example, Greed, Anger and Ignorance are related to CS and accompanied by activities.

XI. COMMUNICATION BETWEEN DIFFERENT MINDS/SOULS

In the PW realm, the two individuals connect through the five senses and CS. When the CS is made, the CS can be expressed by motor activities and emotions. Emotion is the expression of CS through motor activity, and the autonomic system is composed of sympathetic and parasympathetic nervous systems.

In the MW and invisible PW, there is no brain; the interindividual communication is expressed by the Soul, which has the active part as the Karma. Karma is the part of the Mind that copies the data recorded as memory. As a result, the Soul always has a copy of the memory as Karma. So when the Soul leaves the body, the Soul still retains memory and carries it with it. Communication between two individual Souls is the direct communication between the two entities. So, in the world of MW and PW, the two individuals are in direct contact with each other. The Soul can be in direct contact with each other even at distant distances because the Soul has non-local characteristics, as EM does. In the PW, the contact between the two individuals must be through the intermediary of the senses, so the communication is always indirect. Thus, emotional and social relationships in the PW, space, and time play as obstacles that cannot be overcome even with wireless technology. In humans or animals, the Soul is stuck in the brain, unable to express the non-locality property.

Chapter III: UNIVERSE VERSUS MULTIVERSE.

Summary

No one can prove how large the Universe is and how small the particles that make the Universe are. The Quantum particle is very small, and its location or speed becomes uncertain when measured. Therefore, in Schrodinger's imaginary box containing the cat, using Quantum particles to trigger a mechanism that could kill the cat in the imaginary box, no one knows whether the particles could kill the cat or not. Hughes Everett solved the hypothesis using the Multiverse theory. A cat may die in this Universe but live in the other. At the beginning of the Big Bang theory, the physicist thought that the explosion started from a very small point with an enormous amount of energy and then broke out. Gradually, people think that BB starts with emptiness. If it was a vacuum, the BB would not be from a single point but from the whole vacuum transformed into an instant and infinite vast space. So the Universe can be infinite or from billions... Universes at the beginning and became reunited.

Penrose suggested that the Universe after it is shrunk into a black hole, is called Conformal Cyclic Cosmology (CCC). Thus, the Universe can be infinite and begins from infinity. As the Buddha said, there are infinite Universes, and the innumerable Buddha exists from infinity, as much as the sand grains.

The concept of the earth or the visible world of man is only a part of Creation. The visible and the invisible matter are intermixed, so Creation is a fused Multiverse and, therefore, a whole Universe. Creation may have many creatures and lives different than Earth humans; in other words, they may not have made mistakes, so they have not been sent to the world.

Introduction
I. Einstein's Theory of Relativity and Bohr's Quantum Interpretation

How vast the Universe is is hard to tell for sure, but possibly infinite. The astronomer believes it is up to 90 billion light-years wide (light speed). Measurements indicate that this Universe is vast. According to the simple (singular) BB theory, the Universe is formed by expansion from the initial explosion at a small point and spreads forever to this day.

However, as stated above, there is a tendency in both science and religion to believe that the Universe begins from Void/EM. Because the Universe arises from EM, there is no question that something exists before EM. EM is homogeneous, with no time and no space. After the transformation following the explosion, rising thought, or the Holy Spirit movement, the vacuum changes to have time and space. The moment after the EM transformation, there is a generation of time and space and instantaneous expansion. Because of the homogeneity, each point in the EM variation is similar, so the change in the EM is instantly transmitted at the supraluminal speed. So when it comes to BB, the starting point can't be as small as one thinks at first, but rather a round curve like the head of the shuttlecock or badminton ball or even as large as the newly created space. From there, with the broader notion, the whole newly created space is the starting site of BB. In other words, the BB cannot be a singular point but an infinite space that explodes or at least has countless BBs linked together. So either the whole EM develops into one Universe, or multiple BBs are linked into Multiverses but finally linked together, eventually into a Universe as humans know it.

II. The Multiverse of Hugh Everett

In order to better understand the meaning of Schrodinger's box with the cat, in 1955, Hugh Everett III (1931-1982), in his PhD thesis at Princeton, proposed the theory of Many Worlds Interpretation to add a new view to the Copenhagen school on the Quantum interpretation. The theory fell into oblivion for 10 years before being reheated and, discussed and adopted by many physics theorists even after Everett was drunk and disappointed. If the Universe was multi-world, one could imagine that the cat died in this world but lived in the other. It is also unnecessary to imagine the other world in some remote place, but the world is very close to us; that is, the metaphysical world. (*It suggests that readers should spend more minutes and days reflecting on the idea and will find it more reasonable in theory!*)

III. The view of Sir Penrose.
In the last decade, Sir Roger Penrose, an Oxford mathematician, theoretical physicist, and Nobel Laureate in 2020, is only second to Einstein regarding general relativity in cosmology. He proposed a new concept of BB based on his research on the Black Holes. This concept has remained controversial to Cosmological Physicists. In the BB process, the accelerating expansion is followed by the degeneration of all matters, as exemplified by the Proton decay or degeneration of Electrons, and becomes imperceptible. Subsequently, the Universe becomes a massive Black Hole that sucks in everything it touches, in the manner of a gigantic vacuum cleaner of the Universe near the end of its acceleration. The Black Hole will eventually degenerate with the emission of radiation, become empty, and revert to the Original order (likely Emptiness) that will be ready for another cycle. The cycle is called Aeon. Our Universe is, therefore, preceded and followed by other Universes. The concept is called **Conformal Cyclic Cosmology/CCC.** In addition, Universes are multiple.

The Cosmic Microwave Background supports the above concept of CCC, the low Entropy of the Early Universe, and the identification of Hawking's points, which likely represent remnants from the evaporation of a former Black Hole. Other astrophysicists criticize the evidence that the preceding Universe is lacking.
Penrose's CCC is consistent with Oriental philosophy and Buddhism: Only Emptiness/or Creator is the only Oneness. By the universal law, the Universes are regulated by the law of Birth and Death, and impermanence and must enter in the cycle of "Reincarnation/ Samsara

In Buddhism, the age and the magnitude of the Universe are something that is undescribable, as in the many Buddhist sutras like Flower Adornament (Phap Hoa), **Kinh Pp Hoa, QUYỂN THỨ TƯ PHẨM "HIỆN BẢO THÁP" THỨ MƯỜI MỘT (xem tr 103)**

IV. Findings in the Old Testament
In the first place, God created
Day 1 the light,
Day 2 water and expanse (space).
Day 3 land and trees.
Day 4: The sun, the moon.
Right 5: Living animals in water and on the ground
6: human beings and instruction to be fruitful to fill the surface of the Earth.

Human have God's image. Knowing that God is in MW, there is no visible Form, so the man He created carries the Holy Spirit as God is. It is not on this Earth, because the Bible says:
Genesis 6:1 2 God saw how corrupt the Earth had become, for all the people on Earth had corrupted their ways.
A. The Adam Eve family is specifically named Human, but it may not be the only one that God created:
• Genesis 1:28 blessed mankind and said, "be fruitful to fill the surface of the Earth.
• Genesis 2: God planted a garden in Eden, in the east,* and placed there the man whom he had formed.
• The eldest son of Adam and Eve married, Genesis 4. 17), not to say that the wife made the ribs so may belong to another tribe, Adam and Eve had not to give birth to a daughter
• Henoch and many of Cain's sons were taken by God to wherever they didn't know.
• Genesis 6:4 Giants on the Earth in those days—and afterward—when the sons of God went to the daughters of humans and had children by them. They were the heroes of old, men of renown
B. The Garden of Eden is not the only one.
. Adam Eve lived and cared for the garden. Although the Old Testament never mentioned the existence of another garden in

Heaven, when this family was expelled from the garden, another family gave birth to daughters so that Cain could marry.

> C.Genesis 6:1-3 *When man began to multiply on the face of the land and daughters were born to them, 2 the sons of God saw that the daughters of man were attractive. And they took as their wives any they chose. 3 Then the LORD said, ᶻ"My Spirit shall not abide in⸺ man forever, ªfor he is flesh: his days shall be 120 years.*
>
> • Genesis 6:5-7, *And the LORD regretted that he had made man on the earth, and it ᵍgrieved him to his heart. 7 So the LORD said, "I will blot out man whom I have created from the face of the land, man and animals and creeping things and birds of the Heavens, for I am sorry that I have made them."*

• Noah's descendants, who survived the flood, chose Noah to survive because he is the best of you and the ancestor of today's people. Knowing that they will also be very evil

To sum up, he created humanity in His image, that is, with the Holy Spirit. In particular, Adam Eve was named Human. The ancestors and children committed many sins and made so much trouble that God had to use the deluge to destroy them. The Noah family was the best family to be forgiven, but the children of Noah, the human race on this Earth, still committed many sins.

Beyond this Earth, there may be human beings in another world. Old Testament mentioned giant men often choose to marry their daughters. They are God's children, so they are not in this world. Humans represent the flesh part; the spirit will retreat after 120 years. Furthermore, according to the Duality philosophy, besides the Earth, there can be other Earths and different worlds, such as the MW.

V. Buddhism
Buddha proclaimed the dharma the Agama of Mahayana or Nikaya of Theravada in northern India PPennisulaPennisula, embodied himself as a man of the material. Sometimes, Buddha talks about the MW.

Buddhist sutra
Buddha or infinite quantity of light cannot be described in language but can be compared to the multiplication of the light of

the celestial deva and much more light with Photons, as in the passage from the NiKaya:

Long_Discourses_of_the_Buddha (Digha_Nikaya) *Mahapadana Sutta*: The Great Discourse on the Lineage

> *It is the rule, monks, that when a Bodhisatta descends from the Tusita Heaven into his mother's womb, there appears in this world with its devas, maras and Brahmas, its ascetics and Brahmins, princes and people an immeasurable, splendid light surpassing the glory of the most powerful devas. And whatever dark spaces lie beyond the world's end, chaotic, blind, and black, such that they are not even reached by the powerful rays of sun and moon, are yet illumined by this immeasurable splendid light surpassing the glory of the most powerful devas. And those beings that have been reborn there recognize each other by this light and know: "Other beings, too, have been born here!" And this ten-thousandfold world system trembles and quakes and is convulsed. And this immeasurable light shines forth. That is the rule*

(The above paragraph makes people think that there is matter and power to make light other than Photon more than innumerable time brighter)

But this MW is mentioned a lot more in other sutra in Mhayana such as the Flower Adornmentr, Lotus…sutras,. For example, Western Land Many Fragrances world, Wonderful Joy world Crystal Pearl World by Medicine Master Buddha. Particularly Vimalakirti sutra cites the world of Many Fragrances world, where living sentients are good in behavior as opposed to humans in this earthly world.

Chapter IV: VEIL OF IGNORANCE.
Summary

The current Earthly world consists of Photons and other Quantum particles associated with Photons. In the Physical World/PW, materials and organisms are formed by using Photons as building blocks, whereas in MW, the building blocks consist of particles much more delicate than Photons. These particles can be designated beyond Quantum particles that are invisible. As a result, materials or structures in the MW are not visible to human beings. Thus, human abilities are limited since matter built up by particles more delicate than Photons or other Quantum particles much more delicate than Quantum particles, cannot be known by humans. Knowing that sentients in the MW can still be in contact with each other and acquire information from the visible world without the need for the brain. In the PW, sentients need the brain to receive data from the environment of the PW. The brain transforms the incoming data into Consciousness and then exhibits the Consciousness through motor activity such as locomotion, speech, or emotion. Sentients in the PW interact with each other thanks to the motor activities but are unable to interact with the sentient in the MW. So brain is not simply a mirror that reflects information. Data from objects in the PW must be passed through five processes, so-called five skandhas [consisting of Form (object in the environment and five sensory organs), Perception (transmission of data through sensory nerves), Feeling (unconditioned reflex), Transformation (integration of data in the sensory cortex) and Consciousness (comparing integrated data to stored data in the inner Consciousness and referral to the Omniscience)]. In the above process, the attention is critically necessary. Without attention, the incoming data can not be conscious and is stored as unconsciousness. Attention and the above five processes render the original data filtered and distorted. Buddha called it the veil of ignorance. More important than the veil of Ignorance limits information about space and time. veil of Ignorance often makes people deny the MW

Introduction.
The Universe is created from EM initiated by the BB or arising thought or intention of God. EM is uniform and homogeneous, with the potential of unlimited power and ultimate Omniscience. EM is not a void per se but contains beyond Quantum particles so delicate that humans with CS cannot recognize them. So, the Universe includes particles, as described in physics. The smallest particle described in physics is a Photon. Those particles that are smaller than the "massless" Photons cannot be denied. Because it is not visible but exists, it is called MW particle.

I. AFTER THE CREATION.
When disturbed by a thought, non-discriminative EM changes its original status with a loss of characteristics like non-discrimination, non-locality, no time-space...

Right Mindfulness/Right thought creates the MW with form, sound, and other attributes of unimaginable quality, extent, and architecture, eternal life, and everlasting happiness.

False thought or deviated Mindfulness or mistake created PW False thought is not initiated by Creator.

In the Old Testament, Mr and Mrs Adam Eve mistakenly believed that the forbidden fruit was as good as other fruits. After eating that fruit, they were expelled from the Eden Garden. They have to live in a world of hard labor. That is the PW that the Creator created, probably only after there was a sin.

	EM No thought	MW created by Right thought	PW created by False thought
Force	Infinite	Unthinkable omnipotence	Limited
Speed	Instantaneous	Supraluminal	<light speed
Awareness	x	Ultimate Omniscience	Consciousness/CS
Ingniosity	x	Unthinkable	Limited by CS
Perfection	x	Unthinkable	Limited by CS

x; not expressed by EM, only expressed in MW or PW
EM; Emptiness, MW: Metaphysical World, PW: Physical World

The Buddhist sutras also write that False thought arises and causes errors. The original Mind is always neither right nor wrong. Mistakes are from humans. The PW is associated with suffering, hindrance, inversion of concept, and limited awareness with a veil of ignorance. Ignorance is different from intelligence in that knowledge is limited to specific areas of attention.

In Suangama sutra, the Buddha often showed great mercy to humans for the ignorance and the inversion in the PW

II. Veil of Ignorance
The following is a part of chapter I of Surangama Sutra in which Buddha tests his young bother Ananda and the assembly of 1250 attendees about what ultimately generates the vision, thinking, Mind...

> A. Ananda, when you developed that Mind because of the Buddha's thirty-two excellent characteristics, tell me what you saw and loved.
> Ananda replied: World Honoured One, my love came from the use of my Mind, my eyes seeing and my Mind admiring them so that it was set on relinquishing birth and death. The Buddha continued: As you just said, your love was caused by your Mind and eyes, but if you do not know where your Mind and eyes are, you will never be able to destroy delusions. For instance,
> before bandits invade the country, the king should first know where they are before sending his soldiers to destroy them. That which causes you to transmigrate without interruption comes from defects in your Mind and eyes. Now, please tell me where your Mind and
> eyes are. Ananda's replies seven times are wrong.
> 1. In the Body, 2) Outside the Body, 3) Hiding behind the Eyes, 4) Closing the Eyes to See the Darkness as the Seeing in the Body, 5) Thinking as the Mind, 6) Mind Being Interlocked (between the Being and the Man), 7) Unprecedented Mind
>   Finally Buddha said:
> The Buddha said: 'since the time without beginning, all living beings have given rise to all sorts of inversion because of the Karmic seed (of ignorance) which is like the aksa shrub. 9
> This is why seekers of the Truth fail to realize Supreme Enlightenment but achieve only (the states of) sravakas, pratyeka-
> Buddhas, heretics, devas and demons, solely because they do not know the two basic inversions, thereby practising wrongly like those who cannot get food by cooking sand in spite of the passing of aeons as countless as the dust. What are these two basic inversions?
>
> Ananda, the first is the basic root of birth and death caused, since the time without beginning, by the wrong use of a clinging Mind which people mistake for their own nature,
> and the second is their attachment to causal conditions (which screen) the basically bright essence of Consciousness which is the fundamentally pure and clean substance of Nirvanic Enlightenment. Thus, they ignore this basic brightness and so transmigrate through (illusory) realms of existence without realizing the futility of their (wrong) practice. 10
>
> Buddha then held up His golden hued arm and bent His fingers, saying: Ananda, do you see this?
>
> Ananda replied: Yes. The Buddha asked: What do you see? Ananda

> *replied: I see the Buddha raise His arm and bend His fingers, showing a shining fist that dazzles my Mind and eyes. The Buddha asked: How do you see it?*
> *Ananda replied: I and all those here use the eyes to see it. The Buddha asked: You say that I bend my fingers to show a shining fist that dazzles your Mind and eyes; now tell me, as you see my fist, what is that Mind which perceives its brightness?*
> *. Ananda replied: As the Tathagata asks about the Mind and since I am using my own to search for it exhaustively, I conclude that that whic searches is my Mind.*
> *Thinking is unreal*
> *The Buddha said: Hey! Ananda, this is not your Mind.*
> *Ananda stared with astonishment, brought his two palms together, rose from his seat and asked: If this is not my Mind, what is it?. The Buddha replied: Ananda, this is your false thinking which arises from external objects, deludes your true nature and deceives you into mistaking, since the time without beginning, a thief for your own son, thereby losing (sight of) that which is basically permanent; hence the round of birth and death. 11*

Summary: The Original Mind or Ultimate Omniscience /Buddhadhood generates the version. The eye, brain, and thinking Mind play the intermediate role in filtering veils

B. Veil of Ignorance (Fig F9)

The PW with raw matter is another twist that sheds the world of SH on the structure of matter and creatures. Plus, when the human body was created, the brain was made

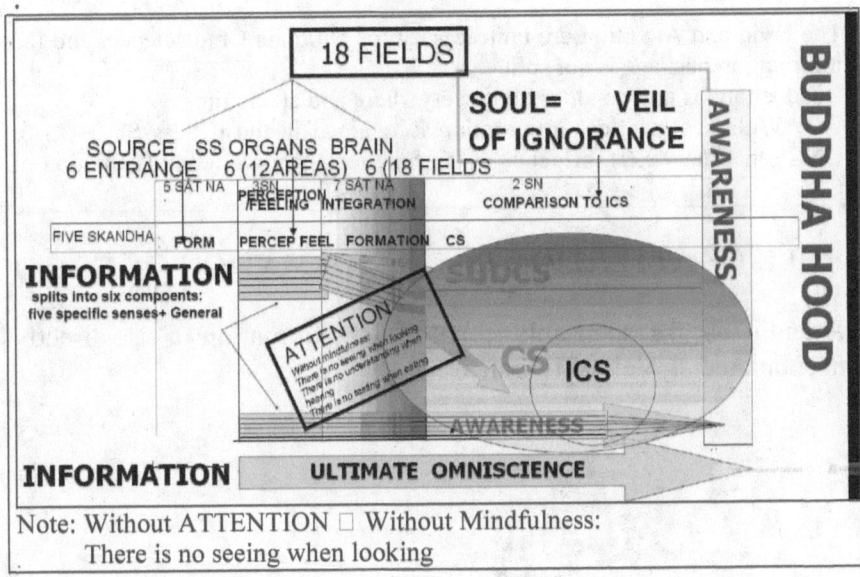

> There is no understanding when hearing
> There is no tasting when eating
>
> *Figure* F9 Diagram showing the original package of input information undergoing two types of modification:
> - Splitting the original package of information into six types of information: five specific sensory organ types and a nonspecific type
> - Filtering effects by five filters
> - Milieu (forming six entrances)
> - Sensory organs (Twelve ayatana, the fusion consisting of six entrance+ six sense data)
> - Feeling: Information triggers a reflex of defense by using the dorsal pathway
> - Formation: integration of information by using the Ventral pathway (Eighteen Fields or realm, the fusion consisting of twelve ayatana+ six types of formation)
> - Consciousness formation by comparing the information in the Ventral pathway to that in the ICS
>
> Therefore, the information undergoes 18 types of filtration called eighteen realms (constituting four steps of filtration) that modify and distort the input. The last step is comparing the data stored in the ICS to label the CS. In the stage of formation, the critical factor is Attention. In the CS labeling, the connection of the ICS with the Ultimate Omniscince/Buddhahood is essential.
>
> In the Formation of Awareness, the original package of information also undergoes splitting into six types. Attention is also necessary, but Attention covers large areas.
>
> The brain and Attention are unnecessary for Ultimate Omniscience, and the information package is not split.
> Buddhahood is universal, present everywhere and at any time
>   Without Attention, information is retained in the ICS as SUB CS or UNCS that may exert influence in the functions of viscera and Formation of CS

ROLE OF ATTENTION IN THE FORMATION OF CS (Fig 10)

Attentin is isdespensable for the CS formation a is directly accountated as Veil of Ignrance

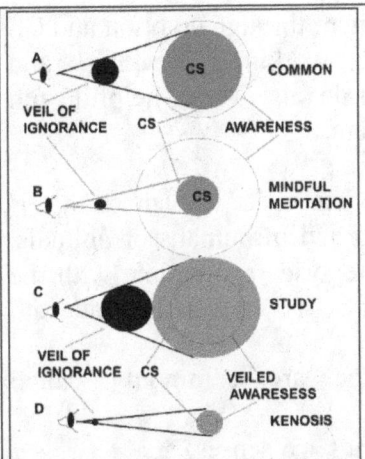

F10 Clear circle: Awareness. Black circle: CS, Gray Circle : Understanding
A: Common
B: Meditation: attention to the restricted target: the understanding is narrower than normal and less detailed. The Awareness is uncovered. If the meditator changes the attention to the areas of Awareness, the Awareness immediately disappears due to the CS involved
C: Learning: increases understanding, obliterated Awareness, and ignorance develops.
D: Kenosis lack of proportional development of Awareness with narrowing awareness

Body and brain are expressed under five Skandhas/Maras: Form, Perception, Feeling, Formation, and Consciousness. These are the intermediate parts between data and the Original Mind (represented by Ultimate Omniscience). Buddha (Buddhahood) does not need to have the five skandhas so that he is in direct contact with data (Buddha regularly meditates to eliminate these five skandhas). For Original Mind, the five Skandhas are the veil of Ignorance represented by the brain or its product, the CS.

So, in humans and animals, the brain and CS are the intermediaries of the UO and the data, whereas, in Buddha, the Knowledge of beings is called a veil of ignorance. UO is the true and complete Knowledge of all things in Creation). In sentients without brains in the Form and No Form realms, the Soul comes in direct contact/connection with other Souls or with the data from the environment. Humans and animals need the brain for UO to reach other creatures and the environment through emotion and CS to perform activities like eating, working, speaking, and communicating. Therefore, the brain is very helpful but significantly hinders the truth of the data.

The original information in nature exists in its wholeness that is undivided. When information is recorded in humans or animals, information must be split into six categories compatible with the five senses of the body and general CS. To convert the data into CS, the information is filtered by:

i. The environment and landscape are commonly called Form/milieu, (six entries)

ii. Perception (12 areas = 6 entries + 6 senses)

iii. Feeling: The mechanism of transfer of information to trigger the corresponding reaction, for example, close your eyes when seeing strange objects flying to the face by using the neuronal dorsal pathway above passing through the movement centers in the brain. This mechanism does not produce CS. So when you close your eyes, you do not know what is flying into your eyes (18 realms = 6 entries + 6 senses + 6 fields).

iv. Formation: the process of integration of information to become CS and emotion by using the ventral neuronal pathway going to the Temporal gyri for audiovisual and other sensory cortices.

v. Consciousness is the process of comparing the input information with the stored information available in the known Inner CS to identify the name or nature of the new data. As a result, the new data is labeled as such. (Note: If the newly integrated information can not be matched with any data in the inner CS, that new information will be updated in the inner CS as part of the learning process.)

C. CS limits the UO.
1 Role Of the Attention in the Generation Of CS

Without attention, data received in the brain is not registered in the CS but recorded in the subCS and even in the Soul as Karmic CS (vn: Nghiệp Thức). It is evident that attention is characterized by heightened levels of neurotransmitters, particularly norepinephrine; glutamate highlights the received data in the cerebral cortex.

2. Changes in the condition of NB due to disabilities, environmental effects such as stress

3. Inner CS is a model of CS the brain retains throughout life, from birth, to compare with newly received information. The Inner Consciousness is specific to each person, affected by the educational environment and family. Therefore, TR has a unique personality for everyone and differs from one person to another. Bodhisatsava Narujana distinguishes three types of Inner Consciousness

11. Parikalpita
/ **vn: Biến kế sở chướng** is wrong discrimination of judgment due to the fabrication from a biased individual Mind and illusional imagination. The views are considered discriminative by the public.

If the ICS is poor in quality, the resulting CS is wrong and biased (in the above example, MM and reference book are inferior in quality, containing inaccurate, insufficient information: the diagnosis is wrong). The encyclopedia is inaccurate, biased, and distorted, leading to the wrong, biased, distorted CS. For example, the yellow color is indicative of the color of death. Similarly, suppose the MM stored in the brain is incorrect. In that case, the Consciousness is biased or based on bad judgment or an imaginative construction of the view that regards the misconception of things as accurate.
Consistent with incorrect, distorted encyclopedia

2. Paratantra (Relative knowledge/ vn: Y tha Sở Tánh):
Suppose the MM and reference books are close to the objective but need to be revised in quality and reflected up to the level of true nature of reality. This is the knowledge commonly known as the common sense of the public. The encyclopedia is consistent common knowledge widely known as the public's common sense.

The two above types of CS are consistent with the concept that "we see things as we are." The view which sees Things as derived. That is not the view which sees things in their true nature.

Literally, "depending on the common sense of the public" is knowledge based on some facts commonly sensed to correspond with the fundamental nature of existence. The characteristic feature of this knowledge is formulated from generation to generation of human beings in the Creation, which is an illusional/ upside down/ inversion world. This world commonly displays illusional views.

- There are seven illusional/ evil views (vn: thất Điên/ skt Viparyaya: Wrong/ Evil / illusional/ misleading views on

1) Permanence   2) Impermanence,
3) Egoism,   4) Non-Egoism,
5) Emptiness   6) Purity and Impurity,
7) Worldly happiness and unhappiness

- There are eight inversions or upside down/ Heretic views/ vn: Bát đảo: wrong views on

1) Permanence   2) Impermanence
2) Non-Egoism   3) Egoism
3) Purity/Tịnh in Nirvana 4) No Purity in Nirvana
4) Pleasure in Nirvana   8) No Pleasure in Nirvana

Consistent with encyclopedia of common sense but still incorrect

3. Parinishpanna

Perfectly-attained knowledge:
Right/ Perfect Knowledge and Suchness/ vn: Viên Thành thật (Tathata) (Samyagjnana) of the five Dharmas, consistent with the concept "we see things as they are." It is available as one reaches the state of indestructible Buddhahood, self-realization beyond Names and Appearances, and all forms of discrimination or judgment.

The thing is perceived as we are. This type of CS of Suchness/ Tathata is only obtained when one reaches the state of Buddhahood, beyond the level of Formlessness, without a Mind of discrimination, and where there is no death, birth or destruction.

This suchness is not perceived through the six senses or cerebral mechanism of integrating the information for CS but is perceived directly at the Buddhahood/ Parinishpanna level. The six senses, brain, and veil of Ignorance (Parikalpita+ Paratantra) distort the information coming from the five senses (However, the brain and the body are necessary for the spirit to communicate with the physical world through the motility-like mental expression, talking, and movement of all parts of the body including viscera.

The encyclopedia is correct.

KURT GODEL'S INCOMPLETENESS THEOREMS AND THE VEIL OF IGNORANCE

In science, mathematics is considered the means by which man expresses the most authentic knowledge of observed events. In Mathematics, accuracy and logic emanate from high-sensitive thinking about nature, the universe, and the world. Therefore, unlike other disciplines of science and logic, such as biology, medicine, philosophy, and other scientific disciplines, mathematics brings the planes, lines, and angles into human life as simple, reasonable, and complete. In addition to reasoning, mathematicians often give the intuitive role an important place in knowledge acquisition. Intuition is the means by which humans perceive nature without inference of the consciousness.

The ancient Greeks considered numbers to have a divine character from the upper level of the universe's knowledge. Mathematics first developed in the Middle East in the 20th century BC, when the Babylonians developed numerology. In China, it is made from the 50th century BC. I ching or Book of Changes, the most ancient Chinese scripture recorded by using the logical symbol of line ___ representing Yang (or positivity) and broken line _ _ representing Yin (or negativity) to predict the behavioral changes of nature and humans. The symbols reflect little of the concept of computation, but mathematics was actually only developed around the 11th century, and geometry was gradually developed. This development was in parallel to Greek mathematics but independently due to language and geographic barriers. Greek mathematics developed from the period of Pythagoras and Plato in the 4th century BC. From the beginning to the present, mathematics has always developed simultaneously with philosophy because of its abstract, practical, and logical character. Then Euclid, in the 3rd century BC, laid the foundation for mathematics with the Euclid proposition, which he thought was obviously unproven. The dominance of geometry makes numerology with integration developed only in the 7th century BC. Perfect and accurate simple reasoning is the characteristic of mathematics for the expression of nature, making it a monotheistic place for its complete and accurate expression compared with other disciplines of knowledge and science. Because of this exclusive position, many mathematicians want to build mathematics not by propositions/axioms but by proven theories. However, they always encounter problems in the above hope because many propositions are easy to accept but cannot be proved by reasoning and cannot be denied. In addition to the Euclid proposition ("a straight line segment can be drawn from any point to any other point" are considered unproven axioms), which he saw as obvious, there are many unproven axioms such as Paul Erdoshave suggested 617 unsolved or incompletely solved problems in 1900, Barry Simon who just have suggested 12 problems in 2000, Jair Minoro Abe, Shotaro Tanaka then Darpa listed more problems in 2001 and 2007.

In 1931, Kurt Gödel presented two theories of the incompleteness of mathematics in the expression of events. Of the two theorems, the one for the event to which the mathematical proposition refers is that it does not include any mathematical problem. The second theory of the facts to which the proposition refers is not integral) Mathematics is not integral and not completely accurate.

While in science and philosophy, the incompleteness of reasoning is common and often acceptable, as in the saying: "Nobody is perfect," it is difficult for anyone, including mathematicians, to accept the incompleteness of this discipline. It has long been the prevalence of word problems that cause paradoxes, such as:
Paradoxe of the liar: I am a liar (then I am not lying!), or
Barber or medical doctor: I only cure a person who can't manage his own disease himself (so does BS cure himself?)

In quantum mechanics, photons or electrons from a system always act the same way because there is " supraluminal communication" (Quantum particle entanglement) even though they are thousands of miles apart. This is the EPR/Einstein-Podolsky/Rosen paradox. The longer people live on this planet, the more paradoxes they create of themselves, according to the principle of Entropy/chaotic level that increases over time.

Therefore, the theory of the incompleteness of mathematics not only affirms the incompleteness of ordinary disciplines of Knowledge, such as the belief in religious and scientific philosophy but also crashes the mathematical logic of mathematics.

The theory that raises the exactness problem of mathematics is only relative. Since mathematics is considered the most precise and logical discipline and also the product of Knowledge, other disciplines of Knowledge, such as philosophy and physics, cannot be entirely accurate and fully encompass all issues.

The theory has proved to have predicted that philosophy and science cannot comprehend all the problems of the universe. Evidence shows that philosophy is always changing in space and time, from ancient to modern. Science has made many mistakes in medicine, physics, and astronomy.
The deficiency of medicine is obvious. Besides the incomplete understanding of malignancies, misunderstanding stomach ulcers has been unacceptable for many decades until the review of H. Pyloi bacteria. The bacteria are obvious in gastric mucosa, which has been blind for decades.

Darwin's tree of evolution is seriously misleading Human, who is the highest form of creatures made by the Creator on this Earth, but it has been mistakenly suggested by an evolutionist researcher as created by a Chimpanzee. (Kien T Mai | Canada (hilarispublisher.com)

In astronomy, the universe concept is constantly changing, and even the Big Bang theory is in question. As for quantum interpretation, the notion that the quantum particle world cannot be affirmed. So, the quantum particles make a strange world separate from the macroscopic world, which was criticized by Einstein, who considered the quantum particle theory incomplete. This imperfection is synonymous with Gödel's incomplete mathematical theory. In Computer Science, Alan Turning (1912 – 7 June 1954), the father of modern computer science, using Gödel's theorem, predicted that computer software, how complete it may be, could be faulty (computer glitch).

Why that? The problem is that because science is the product of Knowledge, it is not complete, and the information is distorted. Maybe the shortcomings are as insignificant as having a small computer error while using. However, incompleteness can be as massive as science, which knows nothing of up to 95% of the universe (including Dark Force). It is only 5% of the universe. It is not to mention that science has misrepresented the universe (as in the world of quantum). Thus, theorems 1 and 2 can be applied to the universe as presented.

As discussed above, CS represents the veil of ignorance that restricts and misrepresents the data of everything (or the Knowledge of all disciplines of CS). As a result, mathematics is also limited and obscured by this veil of ignorance. Another way to decipher the mechanism that creates CS's incompleteness is the CS's standpoint or, rather, the CS's observed position in Creation and the Universe.

CS is the binary view of all problems because humans live in a dualistic world. Knowledge that it is impossible to be consistent but deviated and misguided should be considered both right and wrong. In the dualistic world, there cannot be absolute; as has been mentioned, having happiness must have suffering.

Therefore, when discussing the paradox of "I am a liar, using the Monople /Ultimate point of view is unacceptable because, in the Duality world, there is not the real "I "that is usually oppressed by the false Oneself. The true "I "is the unique standard and serves as a reference system that exists only in the everlasting Reality of the Ultimate Pole. In the Dualistic world, there are two "I: the" true I" is not a liar, and "the false I" is or may be a liar. Therefore, the error committed is mistakenly created by the misunderstanding that EM is always right. In fact, EM is neither Right nor Wrong. Superposition of true and false I render the standard reference a self-reference. This self-reference or self-judgment eventually forms a Paradox, just as the fact of self-proclaiming has created a paradox. In the quantum world, two-photon particles are from a common origin of EM (Singularity). Therefore, separating the two photons is the beginning of the paradox.

In the Gödel theory, the analytical judgment of the mathematician is possible from the hypocritical Self or the rightful Self. Using the rightful Self is correct. However, the rightful Self cannot be used frequently to solve mathematics unless there is a rare event of intuition.

The Gödel theory itself is incomplete.
The Gödel theorem, the judgment of its own scope, should also be trapped in the "logic of the liar": the Gödel theorem itself is neither standard nor integral as it suggests. There is the fact that the incomplete facts of Mathematics (or all disciplines of the Thesis) are incomplete and may be more complete than the original theorem. For example, to make it easier to understand, the Gödel theorem says that 5% of the problem is irrelevant or wrong. When applying the Gödel theorem to the above result, the error could be only 4%. As it goes on, the error will gradually decrease. Of course, it is always greater than zero, not to mention entropy/minority that increases with time, making incompleteness impossible to be nullified. These arguments are expressed through scientific discoveries or breakthroughs that are discovered, with time, in difficult scientific problems or mathematical issues.

With this view, revision to becoming Selfless is the ultimate method (see pages 76-78 of Selflessness) to eradicate the paradox caused by the Gödel theory itself. Egolessnes is paramita (beyond the true shore where there is veil of ignorance), the Ultimate Pole.

After 45 years of Dharma's proclamation in the earthly realm, Buddha said, "I don't say a word" because when speaking to disciples, the word becomes illusional, so the word can no longer be fully expressed in the meaning. Whether it is said or not, the rest is only the meaning of the word.

The whole world is a world of contradictions, paradoxes, and incompleteness. Mathematics can't be an exception to the DualityLaw, nor can it be perfect. This is also the meaning of the world, which is the school of reeducation, which is absolutely not the eternal home of humans, so the integrity of APerfection exists only in the realm of Heaven and Nirvana..

REALITY IN BUDDHISM, DHARMA, ILLUSION AND REALITY IN SCIENCE

The reality in Buddhism: The Truth is that it is unborn and unperishable; it is permanent and exists forever. Thus, in the Creation, only Emptiness/Nothingness is true, all other things are illusional because they represent the reflection from the inner Mind (also called the Inner Consciousness) (please refer to Laṅkāvatāra sutra when Bodhisatsava asked Age of Buddha regarding the Truth and the reflection) (note: Dreams and EM are not tangible to the five senses, but Dreams are illusory because they aren't permanent, EM is real because it is permanent.

DHARMA. The order, law, mechanism, and methods that govern and create the Universe and its attributes, including living creatures from EM . Dharma is expressed in Buddhism, but can also be applied in some other Religions. Dharma can be represented by the quintessential core of the Form it creates. As a result, Form can also be represented as Dharma. Because it is created after the Creation and is associated with Form, Dharma is illusional and impermanent. The commonly cited example is the boat that is used for a river crossing. After the crossing, the boat, which is the Dharma in this case, must be given up. In Agama and Diamond Sutra; Buddha said: Dharma must be given up, so is the unlawful Dharma.

• The interface between EM and the Creation of the dualistic realm. It is the state of Primordial Duality with both characteristics of EM (no discrimination, stillness, no time/space) and Illusion (disturbance, discrimination), both selflessness and self, both Truth and falsehood.

ILLUSION
There is a tendency in Theravada to distinguish two types of Dharmas.

- Dharma of active variant (vn Pháp hữu vi) is the mechanism of making things of the visible world, is illusional and

- Dharma of inactive variant (Pháp vô vi) (distinct from unlawful Dharma), is the mechanism that makes the world of the be further divided:

. From EM with Right Mindful Thought making the Nirvana (Nirvana without reminder), colorless Buddha, can be considered the Truth. No karma is associated

. From CK with False Mindful Thought making the visible world, but in the earliest period, the so-called Primordial Duality, therefore is Nirvana with a reminder, this Dharma is illusional and is associated with karma

The Right Thought) is Dharma secondary to the Creation. It is illusional, the wrong thought that makes this Physical World, which is the world of illusion, upside down.

Lao Tsu said: When the Tao is lost there is virtue. When virtue is lost there is benevolence. When benevolence is lost there is righteousness. When righteousness is lost there are rituals. Rituals are the end of fidelity and honesty, And the beginning of confusion

In this early stage, Dharma played a special role. According to the Mahayana, this Dharma is illusional (because after EM is born) and should also be eliminated. Contrary to Hyayana, this Dharma is true (because it is too close to CK). This concept is practical but not logistical when it comes to Tao.

Consider the following Buddha's saying to determine the viewpoint.

The Buddha said: *A Nan, look at all the Dharmas, are there any that are not perishable? But I've never heard you say EM that is perishable* - Why? Because EM is not created, it cannot be altered. (Note: Law consists of principles, rules, and objects = all that is in creation/Universe).

Reality at the present moment refers to the events and things in the present created by Dharma, like the river mountain, the society looks with an enlightened Mind.

On the contrary, the reality of Science is what can be measured and observed. As is well known by Godel's incompleteness theorem, Science and Philosophy are absolutely unreliable. The measurement is only relatively accurate. Therefore, the reality of Science is completely opposite to that of TAO and is illusional according to TAO (because the Form will be corrupted). Only the non-erring words of the Buddha are credible. Unfortunately, the Holy Scriptures sometimes lack authenticity in the notes; words are difficult to understand, so it is easy to misunderstand (as well, the philosophy—as of Kant—is very difficult to understand and read!). That's not to mention that the Buddha couldn't describe all of His understanding, then, over 2,000 years ago.

The problem is that simple, but when a person lives in a particular pattern and that pattern persists for a very long time, then a person is prone to be mistaken and to let the pattern that he is living be a reality. It is impossible to judge the reality based on the individual view that lives in some model but from the judge who looks from outside the model, ultimately rather than standing on the view of the Supreme or CK. This is also a reasoning: Right or wrong cannot be judged from one's own judgment, but from another independent observer. The only independent is God. In this case, it is the intelligence of THBN.

THBN is the Supreme Mind, knowing everything in the Multiverse. It can be expressed by saying: The big is inside and the small is not outside. Standing on the rational or scientific concept, THBN is the set of all the laws of the universe: CK's Three Self, the Infinite Bowl of Longevity, Bohm's Inner Order (Implicate Order), Supersymmetry in Uniformity, Invincibility in Childhood, Ocean Law, Archimede's Power, Destination to Euclid, Newton's Law of Attraction, Einstein's Theory of Relativity, Godel's Incomplete Theory, Bohr and Heisenberg's Summary Concept, M theory, 11 dimension theory (10 dimensions, time, possibilities, probability...) and spacetime). The synthesis of the appropriate rules of rule is THBN, which is the component of the superior crab. The other part is power.

In summary, the ignorance is due to

1) The construction of the world is based on Photons as basic particles. Although this particle is small, it is not the smallest particle in the Universe. Therefore, it is possible to say that the structure of the world is not delicate enough, so it is impossible to use Photons to compare, see or measure objects or phenomena in the MW.

2. Environment and brain

Due to the veil of Ignorance , humans do not believe in God,

Chapter V: THE METAPHYSICAL WORLD: SIENCE IN IN THE SUPRALUMINAL SPEED AND MIIRACLEs

Summary

From the concepts of plurality and reality, the Universe born after the Big Bang cannot be unique. The existence of the metaphysical world/ MW is essential in conceptual, logical reasoning. If physics has an experimental approach based on wisdom and Knowledge, then mathematics can go beyond experimentation to the highest level of Knowledge. So mathematics can approach the MW. Mathematics suggests virtual numbers with $i^2 = -1$ hay $i=\sqrt{-1}$. Imaginary i is not a reality in the visible physical world; then it is a reality of MW because MW is the opposite of the visible world.

$$Ei = mc^2/\sqrt{1-v^2/c^2}$$

In Einstein's equation ($E = mc^2/\sqrt{1-v^2/c^2}$ 1), when v>c, E becomes a virtual number when applied to the visible world, so E is a virtual number represented by Ei as force.

- Since the Buddha and MW are an invisible entity but not an illusion (like seeing halo or flickering luminous spots of the diseased eyes); this Ei force cannot be the power of Buddha or other sentients in MW.
- Ei corresponds to the Karma caused by the sins of each being.
- Karmas are carried by the Soul. The Soul is an entity having real weight (based on the hypothesis that the Soul is associated with gravity as suggested by Duncan MacDougall).

Moreover, in the equation, when v is stronger, the Karma is lighter or weaker, which means that the less evil the work; when v is slower, heavier is the Soul; when v reaches c, the Karma is too heavy or dense to obscure the light of Heaven oMW, which means the Hell the Heaven /MW light.

Based on the above concepts and hypotheses, the highest world of MW, with no or less Karma, is full of light, as in the case of the world of Buddha. On the contrary, when the Karma is so heavy, MW light is obliterated, and the world will be dark and invisible, such as in the case of Hell. Only the world of humans and animals has both Buddha or MW light (but beings are invisible) and Photons with light made up by Photons that make only PW things visible.

The MW with supraluminal speed is possibly composed of beyond-Quantum particles unknown to Consciousness. The MW is delicate, magnificent, splendid, ingenious, and magical in structure, shape, and sound. Energy and awareness are unlimited (progressing to the state of omnipotence and Omniscience in the full sense).

This world can only be known through high-level divination or through the description in the Buddha sutras or in the Bible. Buddha said that what human beings can realize is simply an illusion, a reflection of Consciousness's misconception. The likeness of the world MW cannot be seen in Buddha's words: *"Whoever seeks me by image or sound is erroneous in practice and cannot meet Buddha."* The MW was the primitive home of man before the ancestors, Mr and Mrs Adam Eve, were driven down from Paradise/Eden Garden to the Earth for re-education.

Introduction
Ancient Buddhist stories tell the following story, copied here as an example of the negation of a true entity the superhumanity of the world as an entity.

Old Buddhist Stories: Turtles and fish

Once upon a time there was a fish, because it was a species in the water, so of course life lived only in the water, and outside the water, it knew nothing. One day he was swimming in the lake, encountering a turtle he had been familiar with before, travelling on land back. He said Hello:
- Hello! I haven't seen you in a while. Where were you once?
- Oh, I traveled from the mainland back. The ground is too dry!
Dry ground? What are you saying weird? I've never seen such a strange place. Is there a dry ground?
- Hey, I'm trying to play again for more logic. I think: your expression is not very clear. Would you please tell me what the land you say is like in our world?
- Is it cool and wet?
- Is it all through so that the light can pass through?
- Is it soft and easy to squeeze so I can swing the microphone and move in it easily?
- Can it move and spill into a waterfall?
- Can it lift up to form the top silver waves?

Turtles answer no to all questions

The fish herself complained: The land you said was not anything I put forward, then the land must not be real.

- Good! I decided there was no land. I can't do anything better because my Mind is slow, just let me continue to believe as I thought. But someday, if there is someone better than I and able to tell you the difference between land and water, you will see that you are just a foolish fish.

The story of the dragonfly

The story is told as an example for babies to explain the departure of the dead. The story was also used by Subrahmanyan Chandrasekhar: the Nobel Prize-winning physicist in physics to describe celestial bodies as they approach a black hole and are sucked into and disappear.
In a pond there is a tribe of larvae with an average lifespan of 2-3 years. Occasionally, the tribe noticed that there was a larvae climbing up the water surface and disappearing, not knowing where it went to live and die. The

> *tribe decided that in the future, if any individual went up to the surface of the water, he promised to return to describe life on the other side of the water.*
>
> *When one larvae was pushed out of the water, he was unconscious for five or six hours, when he woke up he found himself lying on the ground, his body changed with two wings and had an urge to fly. When he was flying into air, he suddenly remembered his promise to the clan to return to his homeland pond to tell the tribe. But when he touches the surface of the water, he can't go under the water, but he thinks that even if he can go under the pond, his friends don't recognize who he is, only he knows that he is the old son. So he flew away to live a happy and fun life in the upper realm for a couple of weeks of life.*

Over the past two centuries, man has made great progress in understanding the Universe and nature. Einstein's theory of relativity and NASA's James Webb Space Telescope (JWST) have opened up a broad vision of the Universe of billions of celestials. Electronic microscopy, chemistry, and biology with molecular analysis techniques, CERN's Large Hadron Collider knocks an atom's nucleus into measurable Quantum particles, the hadron particles. In summary, scientific advances have allowed humans to look far into the Universe for billions of years, up to 300 million years after the Big Bang (compared to the age of the Universe of 13.8 billion years), measuring small energies up to 6.6260701510-34joule-hertz (or Joule-seconds), identifying small Photon particles up to zero weight and the speed of light 300,000km/s.

On the other hand, as the story tells at the beginning of this article, in the metaphysical world described in the classics, the major religions often refer to phenomena that are incomprehensible to the CS. With the veil of ignorance, the above event can be expressed by two typical phenomena that need to be learned, and it is very difficult to explain the mechanism by the CS:
 Supraluminal speed of light and
 Miracle

I. ULTIMATE OMNISCIENCE IN RELIGIONS.
Most people believe in science and deny religion and Spirituality because of the propaganda that science is based on facts, evidence, and the ability to predict accurately. Science denies divinity because divinity is based solely on faith in the Buddha's

Revelation or Old and New Testaments. But think again; science also builds on propositions. Mathematics based on Euclid's proposition reveals many errors in the vast Universe. Modern science is based on Einstein's theory of relativity (that Photons have no weight, m=zero, and have absolute velocity; nothing travels faster than light); science is also based on the "concept" of Quantum (Copenhague's Quantum interpretation) suggested by Bohr of the Netherlands. Bohr and Einstein never agreed on the Quantum world. To say so to see that science, in Essence, is also based on "revelation." The difference between the Spirituality of religion and the achievement of science is the Revelation of the Buddha or of Bohr and Einstein. When Einstein said Photons with no weight should travel the fastest, the conclusion was that it was just a proposed proposition with no preamble. Physicists found that the fastest-moving light was true, but it was true only in science and not for the whole reality of the Universe. Buddha's light shines throughout the vast Universe. The problem is that humans are constituted of elementary particles based on Photons and their electromagnetic activity, so humans can see and sense something that is constituted by Photon-based particles, the Quantum particle.

On the other hand, Buddha is omniscient, has a perfect Mind, and sees all things in the Universe as visible without deviating from a viewpoint, even in the visible and invisible realms. Buddha moves faster than light or has many activities that do not follow the laws of relativity based on electromagnetic waves.

At the time of Buddha, humans did not know what Photons were, so Buddha could not point out the difference between the PW and MW. Today, people know the physical world thanks to the scientific understanding of Photons and electromagnetic waves, but Photons still obliterate the MW. The MW does not contain Photons but has more delicate particles and structures.

The Essence in the revelation in the Testament and Buddhist sutras is never wrong (there is only a misunderstanding or erroneous recording of the sayings in Holy scriptures by the worldly people), but Einstein and Bohr have mistakes (if not mistakes, why are they argued each other until death and don't look at each other). At least one person or both are wrong! With the wrong proposition, the result is only justified within the scope of the proposition; a result from the wrong position can not be used to denounce religion and Spirituality.

Physicists discuss Quantum uncertainty as demonstrated by the inability to determine the position and speed simultaneously. This inability is thought to be due to the characteristics of the Quantum world rather than due to sensitivity in measurement techniques. This demonstrates the scientific subjectivity of many of the characteristics of Quantum. In such a view, David Bohr (in Princeton and London, UK) argues that Quantum may not yet be the limit of the particles of matter in the Universe.

In summary, the divine authority of religion is only the other part of the entity that science cannot see because of the veil of ignorance.

II. THE PHYSICAL AND METAPHYSICAL WORLDS.

As previously stated, the entity consists of the visible part known by the body and the metaphysical part suspected by the indirect effects of this part on the visible part. Religion has a holistic view but its weakness is based on the belief in the revelation of the Creator.

Physics, chemistry and biology can only describe the tangible part. Mathematics based on mathematical inference, based on theory and determination but systematic with tested formulas, can bring people closer to religion. The reason is mathematics by inference, going from the entity of science to the supernatural phenomenon. One of the theories of mathematics, i is a virtual number, with $i^2 = -1$ or

$\sqrt{-1} = i$.

Imaginary is a virtual number that does not exist in reality but can exist in a world beyond reality. The world can only be the invisible/supernatural world. In Buddhist worldview, Karma is an abstract indicator of the material world but has an indirect effect onto the material world. The Buddhist worldview of three Realms composed of: No Form, Form and Passion Realms. Only the PW of humans and Animals is both visible and metaphysical. In the Passion Realm, the levels of Hungry Ghost and Hell are invisible because the DM infers darkness; there is no Photon/electromagnetic energy, therefore the insensitivity to the five senses (invisible). But these levels t should probably not be called the MW, because they are below Man's level.

The Karma brings the Soul down from the MW from NoForm Realm ☐ Form ☐ Passion Realm. (Deva☐ Asura ☐ Humam ☐ Animal ☐ Hungry Ghosts –Hell) . Karma brings humans levels of Hell and Ghosts. In other words, true force or energy and the virtual force help people live in the PW. The virtual force expressed by the Ei is the motive to degrade the Soul.

III. TRAVEL WITH SUPRALUMINAL SPEED

It is a well-known concept in Buddhist sutras that Buddhas, Bodhisattvas, and the Spirit/Soul in the metaphysical realm manifest almost instantaneously at a meeting convened by Buddha Shakyamuni. This paragraph discusses this paramount issue. This book proposes the idea that the Soul is primarily composed of Dark Matter (DM). If supported by related facts or concepts, this proposal could reinforce our understanding of the Soul, its composition, and its manifestation in the metaphysical realm. Despite the elusive nature of DM in all investigations and the hypothetical status of dark Photons, a particle of DM, according to special relativity theory, the possibility of particles faster than light has been repeatedly proposed, albeit mainly in fiction, since the early 20th century.

Recently, the hypothesis of the particle Tachyon, which is related to DM, re-emerged. Based on the equation:

$E = mc^2 / \sqrt{1-v^2/c^2}$

$E = mc^2 / \sqrt{1-v^2/c^2}$

If $v=0$, (object not moving) $E=mc^2$, the famous Einstein formula

If $v > c$,

$\sqrt{1-v^2/c^2}$ is an imaginary number (represented as i with $i^2 = -1$).

It is currently believed that for E to be a real number, m should be an imaginary number. Of particular interest, for a fixed m, the faster this imaginary m travels, the smaller the energy E becomes. This intriguing scenario does not align with the current concept of physics and spirituality.

It is also commonly believed that an imaginary number is an integral part of an entity, although this part is not within the domain of attention and, therefore, beyond Consciousness (CS). For physicists, reality consists of all data accessible to the CS, and unreal or illusional/imaginary data are not accessible to the CS (meaning unmeasurable, unobservable….by five sensory organs).

As pointed at the beginning of this book, everything exists in its wholeness, including the physical and metaphysical parts. Therefore imaginary number:

$\sqrt{1-v^2/c^2}$ may represent entities in the metaphysical realm. In the metaphysical realm, the Soul, which is mainly composed of DM, is imaginary to physicists; the energy E associated with the Soul is characterized by the CS, which is also Karma. Karma manifests by its Karmic energy. However, in the metaphysical realm, the Soul with its DM is suspiciously associated with gravity, which accounts for the real mass m. Therefore mi=m (imaginary mass). As a result, E in
$$E = mc^2 / \sqrt{1-v^2/c^2}$$
must be imaginary. One can consider Ei to replace E in the above equation, that is, imaginary; Ei can be expressed as:
$$Ei = mc^2 / \sqrt{1-v^2/c^2}$$

According to Einstein's Relativistic theory, the Photon represents the hallmark particle without mass (m=zero) (and is associated with a travel speed of 300 km/msec, representing the upper limit of all speeds in this Universe). Suppose one considers the zero mass as an assumption that results from the limited capability of the human brain's Consciousness, the zero mass only represents the inability of the human brain to this measurement beyond that threshold rather than the reality of the Creation. In other words, zero mass of Photons represents the limit of the physical world. Beyond these zero limits is the metaphysical realm. The reason is that nothing can be measured below m of the Photon, which does not mean nothing exists.

Therefore, in keeping with Einstein's Relativistic theory, m or E beyond this human CS limit is called imaginary (or illusional). (Of note: m of the Soul is both real because it is hypothetically measurable and unreal because it is still not accessible to the CS)

Table: Grading the Soul in different metaphysical and physical realm according to Karmic energy and corresponding Soul speed

Immateral Realm.ealm (Realm of Passion
/No form/Noorm
Beauty/pure spirit Matter/Beaut

Metaphysical	Meta physical	Metaphysical	Physical & Metaphysical	Meta physical
Dhyana:4. Arahat Buddha	Dhyana: 1,2,3.	Asura, Deva (state of God)	HUMANS, Animals	Hungry Ghosts, Hell
No more Karma		Decreased Karma ☐	Real energy and Karma For living	☐ increased Karma $v\downarrow$ with $Ei\uparrow$
$v\uparrow$ with $Es\uparrow$ and		$v\uparrow$ with $Ei\downarrow$		

v supraluminal velocity of the Soul, Es Energy oh the Soul, Ei: imaginary Energy or Karma

In the metaphysical realm, if m represents the mass of the Soul, Ei must represent the Karmic Energy. Karmic energy, or simply Karma, is the critical factor that drives the Soul in the transmigration, the motivation of sentient beings in action in living, and exerts influence on the energy for theSoul travel.
$Ei = mc^2 / \sqrt{1-v^2/c^2}$

According to Buddha, in worldly life, sentient beings continuously create and accumulate Karma, which results in the inversion or turmoil of the Creation. Therefore, Karma, which is nothing but Consciousness, a veil of ignorance, deviates, distorts, and obliterates Buddhdhood and Omniscience. As a result, Karmic energy renders the Soul downgrading on the spiritual scale. One can express this phenomenon of obliteration by this equation with Eo, the original energy assigned to each Soul, and Es, the current energy of the Soul after the obliteration by the Karma or Consciousness

$$Es = Eo - Ei = Eo - mc^2/\sqrt{1-v^2/c^2}$$

The equation denotes those entities with higher energy travel faster. The more enlightened the spirit, the more energy it has and the faster it travels. This could have profound implications for our understanding of energy, spirit/Soul, and enlightenment. Supraluminal travel only applies to entities in the imaginary/metaphysical realms. In the physical realm, this type of supraluminal communication may be possible in humans with high levels of enlightenment whose spirit can detach from the physical body (similar to cases of out-of-body experience). Nevertheless, non-enlightened humans can also communicate with bodiless Souls or spirits, as in instances of mediumship.

In the above equation, if v decreases to c, Ei becomes very high in value and will obliterate the Buddhahood/Holy Spirit. If v approaches zero value, Ei=E=mc2). This is consistent with the fact that Karma originates from Physical material and is the direct cause of Greed and Anger/ Renouncing worldly things is the decent road to the spiritual life. In other words, Karmic energy is materialistic. The evidence is overwhelming: Buddha left his golden throne, palace, precious stones, and jewelry to live in the forest and beg for daily food, just enough for survival. In the Old Testament, the fact that Adam and Eva, who ate the fruit in the middle of the Eden garden, were expelled from Heaven represents the message of the Bible, which instructs that Materialistic things are the boulevard to Hell. The metaphysical world consists of the Realm of no Form, the Realm of Form, and part of the Realm of Passion. Only the Physical Realm, to which humans and all animals belong, has Photons. The Hell represents the Realm of Invisible Form, inaccessible to the five sensory organs due to the lack of Photons and is dark due the obliteration of the heavenly light by the high level of Ei (Karma)/DM. The Hell likely belongs to the metaphysical Realm. The metaphysical realms do not have Photons and are likely characterized by other particles carrying the energy (for example, the hypothetical Dark Photons or Tachyons). The later particles do not interact with Photons but use other gauge systems. As a result, dark matter and dark Photons can not be characterized, but they can indirectly affect the Photons, like deviating from visible light or interacting with the Physical realm through the brain at the level of neuronal synapses. As a result, visualization of the metaphysical realm is not possible through sensory organs but only by discarding the veil of Ignorance (example: through meditation).

Diagram Showing the Relationship of Buddhahood, Karma, and Velocity in Different Realms of the Creation

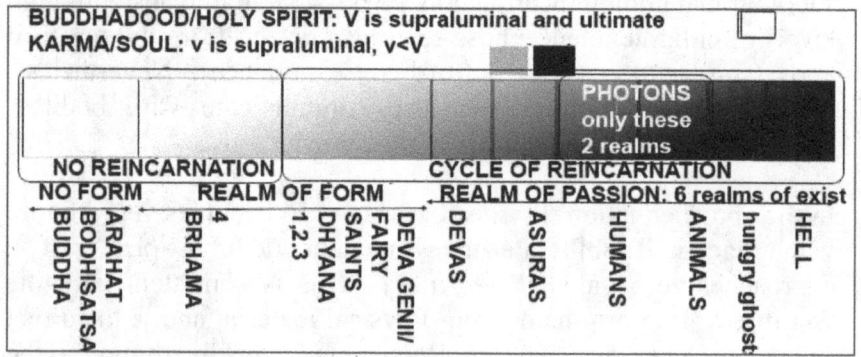

Darker shade, lower supraluminal velocity v

MATTER IS The KARMA

Can be suggested in the following paragraph of Testament

> Luke 16:22-30
>
> [22] "The time came when the beggar died and the angels carried him to Abraham's side. The rich man also died and was buried. [23] In Hades, where he was in torment, he looked up and saw Abraham far away, with Lazarus by his side. [24] So he called to him, 'Father Abraham, have pity on me and send Lazarus to dip the tip of his finger in water and cool my tongue, because I am in agony in this fire.'
>
> [25] "But Abraham replied, 'Son, remember that in your lifetime you received your good things, while Lazarus received bad things, but now he is comforted here and you are in agony. [26] And besides all this, between us and you a great chasm has been set in place, so that those who want to go from here to you cannot, nor can anyone cross over from there to us.'
>
> [27] "He answered, 'Then I beg you, father, send Lazarus to my family, [28] for I have five brothers. Let him warn them, so that they will not also come to this place of torment.'

> [29] "Abraham replied, 'They have Moses and the Prophets; let them listen to them.'
> [30] "'No, father Abraham,' he said, 'but if someone from the dead goes to them, they will repent.'

IV. MIRACLES IN THE MW.

. The spiritual phenomenon.
- There are many examples, such as Nostradamus, the prophets predicting events in the remote immediate or future, and the pandemic, but it is hard to verify.
- Cases of finding remains of soldiers who died in the Vietnam War, such as Mrs. Phan Thi Bich Hang, Hoang Thi Them, Doan Viet Tien... and many others.
- The phenomenon of NDE and OBE
- Jesus walks on the water, making wine, fish, and bread and healing the blind.
- Buddha went up to Tusitiva and preached to his mother. Countless unthinkable lands are described in various Sutra Flower Adornments, Lotus. Bodhisattva Nagarjuna went to Naga realm (to learn the Mahayana sutras hidden in the Oceanic Royal Palace)
- A case on CNN.

Baby who survived car crash into Utah river gets better

> The story was told by CNN in March 2015: Last night, the 25-year-old mother of GLJ, who was driving on the road along the banks of the Spanish Fork River in Utah, carried her 18-month-old daughter L in the back seat. Unfortunately she lost the control when crossing the river, and caused the car to crash into the river waves. The car sank, the cold water of the river. It was only the next morning that a local man came to the river and discovered it, and he hurried for help.
>
> When the first four rescuers arrived at the scene, it was 12 hours since the car was drown. Looking at the situation of the car flooded deep in the water with the skin cut cold, they assumed that no one survived so intended to turn up to call the truck to tow the car, then suddenly they heard the woman crying out of the car "Save my baby with!"
>
> All four rescue workers heard clearly, they stared at each other and turned around, When they break the glass of the car it was miraculous, although the mother was dead, but the little girl L, stuck in the safety chair, was still alive, but unconscious and. Lily was rescued and after a few days in the hospital, she returned home

> *"The four of us heard a distinct voice coming from the car,"* Warner told CNN. *"To me, it didn't sound like a child's voice."*

A non-enlightened Soul can enter a normal person's brain to convey information. It is called an illusion, but the event is a spiritual and materialistic process.

In Buddhism, at large meeting, Buddha also non-enlightened people such as A-nan to hear the Buddha from all over the Universe; the process is to help the brain of the normal person to contact the Spirits in the higher world.

In the phenomenon of Our Lady of Fatima in Portugal or in La Vang, Our Lady has manifested herself in the Minds of those who need to be manifested. Expression like above cannot be recorded by a video or audio recorder. Similarly, if the UFO status is real, only the person who sees can know but can not record images or sounds by machine.

In the case of Jesus resurrecting Lazarus after four days of death, the Lord (God representing him) made the image of Lazarus incorporated into the brains of the witnesses, even the last time Lazarus sat at the last dinner table with the Lord. However, Lazarus' body was dead, not living like a normal man without God. God said Lazarus was a good man who did not deserve to die. Death here is spiritual blindness, so there will be life in Heaven. Sound light and objects such as gemstones, diamonds, castles in the metaphysical realm are also expressed according to the laws of Creation that created the Universe.

To summarize, mystery or miracle is the ability of the Spirit that a secular person with a high level of CS can hardly understand. However, the miracle mechanism also follows the laws of physics and extends into the metaphysical realm. This law may be slightly modified, so it may be slightly different from the visible world, but it must be based on the fundamental principles of Creation. The breakdown and re-synthesis of the atomic molecules of the body of the deceased must follow the process of biochemical physics and spiritual attachment of the Soul to the body. The Buddha often says that sand cannot turn sand into rice. Similarly, the mystery of prayer can only be expressed through forms of reality; for example, the sick who pray should be saved often, as well as through medical treatment.

Through supraluminal velocity and the Karma, the MW is the opposite of this PW. Though opposite, the two realms represent the seamless extension of one from the other. The interruption between the two worlds is a hallucination caused by the brain constructed specifically for PW. In the PW, Photons are the measuring tool for objects in this visible world. Know that Photons may not be the only measuring tool in the other world of Creation. The MW has no Photons, so human senses cannot perceive it. Because of the MW, there are no Photons, so the beings of the PW can't perceive the data from MW. But the MW also has mountains but higher (like the Tu Di mountain), there is the ocean where the Oceanic King was mentioned in the Flower adornment sutra, the continent with beautiful flowers, there are diamond flowers, gems but more attractive, the magnificent scenery, there is a more magical sound.... This is because, in the MW, the speed is faster, the energy is more enormous, the structure is more sophisticated, and the life of beings is longer. As previously stated, the brain, with the neural synapses, is the site of communication between PW and the Soul. The Soul belongs to the MW. Therefore, the brain is an essential mediator of the MW and the PW and helps humans know the MW's presence through a phenomenon known as miracles. This mysticism should be seen as the natural reality of the superworld. In other words, to insert an image (or other types of data) into the Consciousness, it is simply insert the image into the Soul (known as belonging to the MW)

In the metaphysical realm, Photons in the visual realm are possibly replaced by smaller particles than Photons. Photons with no weight represent the lowest limit of human CS. The simple reason is that what humans do not identify cannot be said to be nonexistent. For example, the vacuum of the PW that CS cannot identify. Because the veil of Ignorance limits CS.

The idea above, the scientific investigation of the MW, finds only indirect evidence. The indirect evidence is that we know many spiritual phenomena that science has always denied because of prejudice and hypocrisy. The desire to discover direct evidence of the MW is an impossibility if not through enlightenment by Meditation or by a state that has a special ability to communicate with the Soul in awakening. Since the suspicious Dark Substance is the underlying substance for the Photonless Soul, the same is true for the Dark Force, which occupies more than two-thirds of the Universe. Artificial intelligence (AI) today helps people to progress technically and get lost in magic, but the speed of light limits it, so it is impossible to go beyond this limit to enter the spiritual world. Meditation is the way back to "real life", which can help people be truly happy because they understand that life is complete only with "reality" and spirituality.

However, when praying for the help of God or Buddha, it is that the God or Buddha wants to let everyone know about the world of MW and the Spiritual power so that people learn and know that the MW is the eternal home. The Buddha did not give anyone his help and did not deliberately show up.

V. The meaning of praying.
MW is present worldwide, but people in PW cannot see it. Contrarily, sentients in the MW recognize the PW regardless of Photons. Suffering or hindrances are intentional setups of PW. Praying to avoid suffering can go against the meaning of the PW.

Occasionally, the Buddha helps with prayer because the Buddha wants to let people know about the MW and the spiritual power of the Mind so that people learn and know that the MW is the eternal home. The Buddha did not give anyone his help and did not deliberately show up.

VI. The character of the MW.
MW is unrecognizable because the data is not sent through Photons or phenomena related to Photons, such as electromagnetic waves, weak forces, strong forces, and Higgs bosons.

MW manifests through
1. Supraluminal velocity, as described above, the faster the speed, the faster the information leads to the state of space and time and approaches EM (without time and space).

2. objects linked to each other as a Quantum particle and information related to each other through the speed of supraluminal speed so that the difference or distinction between objects is gradually reduced

- Energy: In the example, dividing small objects into "beyond Quantum" particles is the same process as making atomic particles into Quantum particles. The process will generate energy. The more delicate the particles, the greater the energy. The following equation can express the energy above.

v is the speed of the object/data.

$$Es^2 = Eo^2 - Ei^2 = Eo^2 - mc^2/\sqrt{1-v^2/c^2}$$

where E is the energy of the Soul, Eo is the energy of the Buddha (or EM), Ei is Artificial, c is the speed of light

The greater the energy, the more magnificent the structures of the MW.

4. The MW world has no Photons, but there is Buddha's light (often called infinite light), which is much brighter than the light based on electromagnetic waves. Buddha light cannot seen by using CS to observe because CS is not delicate and compared to the Ultimate Omniscience of the MW. UO exists in humans and animals but is masked by the brain/veil of ignorance. Meditation is the solution to cleaning out NB's Karma

5. UO and those living in the MW world can be known through Buddhist sutras.
a) Christianity, typical of the Revelation section of the New Testament, St. John describes God, the Angel, and the magical scenery and sound.
b) Buddhism like Flower Adornment and Lotus sutras.

I. The Flower Adornment.

At the beginning of the scriptures, it is said that 5000 Buddhists are incredibly afraid to leave the meeting. Buddha also finds it difficult to explain miraculous phenomena to the attendant, so he does not want to speak out because he causes doubts in the audience.

In the example of the story, the chief pretends to have a child living in his luxury house, but the house is burning.

> **Chapter XI**
> **The Appearance of a Jeweled Stupa**
> At that time there appeared before the Buddha a seven-jeweled stupa, five hundred yojanas in height and two hundred and fifty yojanas both in length and width, which emerged from the ground and hovered in the air. It was adorned with various jewels, had five thousand railings, and thousands of myriads of chambers. It was decorated with innumerable flags and banners and hanging jeweled necklaces, and myriads of koṭis of jeweled bells hung from the top. The fragrance of tamāla leaves and sandalwood trees exuded from all sides of the stupa, covering the world. The banners and umbrellas were composed of the seven jewels such as gold, silver, lapis lazuli, motherof-pearl, agate, pearl, and ruby; and they rose as high as the palaces of the world-protectors of the four quarters.
> The thirty-three devas rained down Heavenly māndārava flowers in homage to the jeweled stupa. The other thousands of myriads of koṭis of humans, and such nonhumans as devas, nāgas, yakṣas, gandharvas, asuras, garuḍas, kiṃnaras, and maho ragas also respected, honored, revered, and praised the precious stupa by offering all kinds of flowers, perfumes, necklaces, flags, banners, and music.
> Then a tremendous voice issued forth in praise from the jeweled stupa, saying: "Splendid, splendid! O Śākyamuni! The Bhaga vat teaches the Lotus Sutra to the great assembly: the instruction for bodhisattvas and treasured lore of the Buddhas, which is the wisdom attainable by every sentient being! Just so! Just so, O Śākyamuni Bhagavat! What you teach is true!"
> Thereupon the fourfold assembly saw the great jeweled stupa hovering in the air and also heard the voice that issued forth from the stupa. They all were pleased with the teaching and marveled at this unprecedented experience. They stood up from their seats, honored Śākyamuni with their palms pressed together, and withdrew to one side. At that time there was a bodhisattva mahāsattva called Mahā pratibhāna who, realizing that the devas, humans, and asuras of the entire world were puzzled, addressed the Buddha saying: "O Bhagavat! Why has this jeweled stupa emerged from the earth? And why has this voice come forth from it?" Then the Buddha told Bodhisattva Mahāpratibhāna: "The Tathāgata is in this jeweled stupa. In the remote past, immeasurable, incalculable thousands of myriads of koṭis of worlds away in the east there was a land called
> Ratnaviśuddha. In that land there was a Buddha called Prabhūtaratna. When this Buddha was practicing the bodhisattva path in his previous lives he made a great vow, saying: If I become a Buddha, after my parinirvāṇa if the Lotus Sutra is being taught anywhere in all the lands of the ten directions, my stupa shall appear there so that this sutra may be heard, and in order that I may
> bear testimony to it and praise it with the word "Splendid!" "After the Buddha had perfected the path and immediately before his parinirvāṇa, he addressed the monks among the great assembly of devas and humans, saying: After my parinirvāṇa anyone who wishes to pay me homage should build a great stupa! "If there is anyone teaching the Lotus Sutra anywhere in the worlds of the ten directions, this Buddha makes a jeweled stupa emerge out of the ground in that place through his transcendent powers and the power of his vow. He is in the stupa giving

> *praise with the words, 'Splendid, splendid!'* "*O Mahāpratibhāna! The Tathāgata rabhūtaratna has now emerged from the earth, within his stupa, so that he may hear the Lotus Sūtra and give praise with the words, 'Splendid, splendid!'*" *At that time Bodhisattva Mahāpratibhāna spoke to the Buddha through the Tathāgata's transcendent powers, saying: "O Bhagavat! We all want to see this Buddha's form."*
> *The Buddha answered Bodhisattva Mahāsattva Mahāprati bhāna, saying: "This Buddha Prabhūtaratna made a great vow, saying: Whenever my jeweled stupa appears in the presence of a Buddha in order to hear the Lotus Sūtra, if that Buddha wants to show my form to the fourfold assembly he should gather into one place all his magically created forms that are teaching the Dharma in the worlds of the ten directions. After that my form will appear.*
> *"O Mahāpratibhāna! I shall now gather all my magically created forms who are teaching the Dharma in the worlds of the ten directions."*
> *Mahāpratibhāna spoke to the Buddha, saying: "O Bhagavat! We also strongly wish to see the Bhagavat's magically created forms, to honor and pay homage to them!"*
> *Then the Buddha emitted a ray of light from the tuft of white hair between his eyebrows; and they immediately saw the Buddhas in five hundred myriads of koṭis of nayutas of lands in the eastern direction equal in number to the sands of the Ganges River. In these lands the soil was of crystal and adorned with treasure trees and jeweled garments; and these lands were full of innumerable thousands of myriads of koṭis of bodhisattvas. Jeweled drapes were hung everywhere and were covered with jeweled nets. All the Buddhas in these lands were teaching the Dharma in most harmonious voices. They also saw immeasurable thousands of myriads of koṭis of bodhisattvas, filling all the lands and teaching the Dharma to sentient beings. The other directions to the south, north, and west, the four intermediary directions, and the upper and lower regions were also illuminated by the ray of light emitted from the tuft of white hair between the Buddha's eyebrows; and they were also exactly like this. Then all the Buddhas in the ten directions each addressed the assembly of bodhisattvas, saying: "O sons of a virtuous family! We will now go to the place where Śākyamuni is in the sahā world and pay homage to the jeweled stupa of the Tathāgata Prabhūta ratna." At that time the sahā world was immediately purified; the earth was of lapis lazuli, adorned with jeweled trees, its roads laid out like a chessboard and bordered with golden cords; and there were no villages, towns, cities, oceans, rivers, mountains, streams, forests, or groves. Very precious incense was burning, māndā rava flowers were spread everywhere on the earth, and it was covered with jeweled nets and drapes from which jeweled bells hung. With the exception of this assembly the devas and human beings were all moved to other lands... ...*

The wrote Buddha had been enlightened for numerous thousands of trillions years. According to astronomical physics, the Universe is 14 billion years old. But according to Sir Penrose and the philosophy of extinction, the Big Bang is a continuous cycle birth and death, so the age of Creation is extremely long. The jewellery tower is very large, there is a sound from the tower with countless Buddha Buddha...

Chapter XVI, The Lifespan of the Tathāgata-

> *Then the Buddha addressed the assembly of the great bodhisattvas, saying: "O sons of a virtuous family! I will now explain it clearly to you. Suppose all these worlds, whether or not a particle was left in them, were reduced to particles, and each particle represented a kalpa. The period of time since I became a Buddha would exceed this by hundreds of thousands of myriads of koṭis of nayutas of incalculable kalpas. Since then, I have constantly been residing in the sahā world, teaching the Dharma and inspiring sentient beings. I have also been leading and*

> *benefiting sentient beings in incalculable hundreds of thousands of myriads of koṭis of nayutas of other worlds*

The Buddha has gone down to earth many times but didn't stay long because staying long means people will not see love, so they will not learn.

In Lotus sutra, Budha proclaimed the dharma in the oceanic royal palace, which should be correctly conceived that the palace is in the MW, not in the ocean of the PW..

VI. The character of the MW.
When meditating, closing eyes, and being Mindful, attention and Consciousness (the veil of ignorance) are focused on a predetermined target (respiration rate or a certain point of the face. With attention, the neuronal dorsal pathway in the brain is dominated by the CS, and the ventral pathway, due to minimal attention, should see the Light or hear the Sound. This Light is more magical than Photon light and is only revealed when CS is reduced to the minimum so that it can not block the Buddha's Light or Sound from UO.

In other MW images, such as miracles, in the person who sees the Buddha's Light of Nirvana, CS (Photon-based) is temporarily inhibited (probably through the vmPFC/Third eye)

V. BUDDHA'S LIGHT OR INFINITE LIGHT EXPERIENCED IN THE MEDITATION.
VI. THE PURE LAND OF AMITABA BUDDHA and WESTERN WORLD OF ULTIMATE BLISS.
The Universe is vast and pluralistic. So does the MW, which includes many worlds with different states and worlds with both sufferances and pleasures

The Pure Land world is peaceful, with long-lasting happiness; the sentient has a beautiful body, a high level of morality, a determined bodhi Mind, reproduction by transformation (not by sexual conception between Male and Female, no re-incarnation (samsara), possession of six kinds of miraculous spiritual power.

The kingdom comprises gardens made of gold, gems, fresh trees, and without war.

Earthly humans who remember and repeat the name of Amitaba with no disturbed Mind can be liberated and reborn to this land after death. It is divided into three parts, one of which is divided into another three parts; as a result, there are nine parts in total.

Further reading
Amitabha/ Amita Buddha/ Buddha of Unlimited Light. /Buddha of Boundless Light/ Buddha of Irresistable Ligh is very popular in China, Vietnam, Japan and Korea. He is the chief of the Western Pure Land, belonging to another system of worlds distinct from this system of world for innumerable thousands of year. The Amitaba Pure land is obtained thanks to innumerable Buddha's merit
He was a king named Dharmākara who was impressed by a high court official under his rule becoming Buddha.. With vows to give up his throne if he can be offered a land with 48 aspirations that any being in any Universe desiring to be reborn into the Western pure land (vn: tịnh độ) and having faith and sincerity and reciting it for even only ten times, will be guaranteed rebirth Amitaba's land or may I not gain enlightenment, The other vow promises is that he and his bodhisattvas (Amitaba Triad: with two assistant bodhisattvas, usually Avalokiteśvara (vn: Quan Thế Âm Bồ Tát) on the right and Mahāsthāmaprāpta [vn: Đại Thế Chí Bồ Tát] on the left.) will appear before those who, at the moment of death, call upon him.
The Amitaba Pure land is full of splendor with infinite light, sound, precious gems, gold, happiness, joy with long lasting life and are free of worry and illness

---

Eternal life, infinite merit of virtue, and Buddha's light or infinite light are phenomena that cannot be described in language but can be compared to be unnumerable times multiplied by the life, merit of virtue, and light of Photons.

VII. THE WORLD OF DUALITY: NIRVANA OR HIGH LEVEL OF HEAVEN.

The diagram shows that Nirvana, the entity characterized by the development of space and time intermediate between EM and the Creation of the Universe (with the Duality principle), needs to receive more attention or analysis. This can be designated as the Primordial Duality during the first $0-1.10^{-43}$ seconds after BB. The Primordial Duality shares the characteristics of EM and the newly created Realm of Duality. In reality, Primordial Duality is Nirvana or the High level of Heaven. Therefore, spiritual practice does not lead to EM/nihilism but to the original Mind, which has UO and unlimited power (as mentioned in Flowers Adornment, Lotus sutras). Because EM after BB or False or Right Thought/Mindfulness, EM is destroyed. Therefore, there is no more EM after the Creation. It is wrong to assume that spiritual practice led to nothingness and void per se, a wrong nihilistic concept that does not exist in Buddhism and, in general, religion.

A. NIRVANA (Fig 11)

As conceived above, Nirvana is not a fantasy or illusion but an entity. It is not wrong to assert that Nirvana is more realistic than the PW /earthly World. Why that?

First, define what reality is and what illusion is. It is a case of recognizing an object or an event. Only what is unborn and unperishable is permanent: it is EM. Next, what is close to EM is very long-lasting. On the contrary, what is perishable, like the dualistic World (the PW), is impermanent. EM and Nirvana are real because they are recognized as Buddhahood or UO. On the contrary, a thing in PW (in the realm of Duality) is perceived through the brain as equivalent to the reflection of CS rather than recognizing the thing as it is.

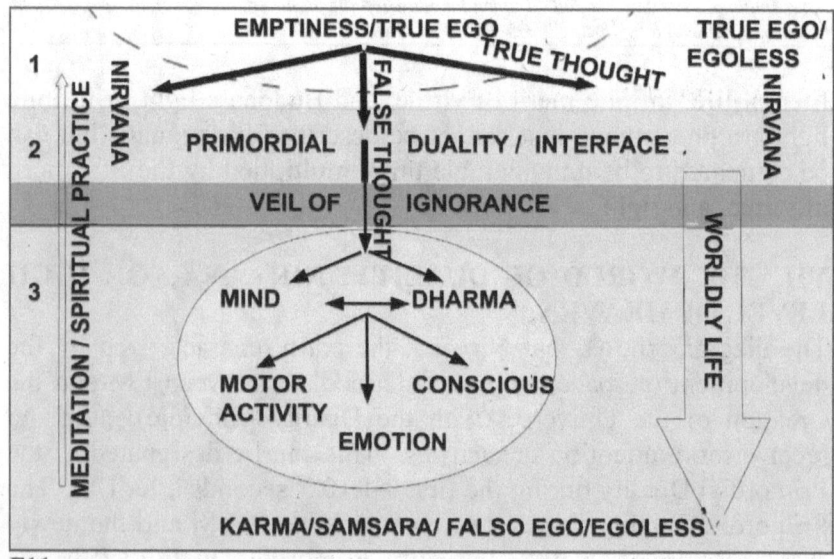

F11

The diagram shows three processes.
  Emptiness (with self/ego)
  (3) The Creation is made by memory and decision/False thought (if by Right Thought there is only Nirvana. If by mistake/ignorance, the visible world/PW is created, the Veil of Ignorance will thicken.

(2) *Primordial Duality: the intermediate between the Emptines/Emptines and the Creation of PW by False thought reflects the Duality principle, i.e., PW and Nirnana. After thought (decision or thought), EM is disturbed and creates space and time*

From EM in the forward (downward) direction creates Dharma and Discriminative Mind/CS. The Original Mind is obliterated and manifested as CS, and Emotion becomes thicker. The backward/upward direction is represented by spiritual cultivation and meditation. The PW is the world of suffering as a learning tool for training and the re-education of the human Mind. Nirvana, or the high level of Heaven, is very close to the original EM; there is no suffering, so there is forever happiness.

Pathway from top down or bottom up to the right is seamless and uninterrupted phenomenon. So, when the physicist says that Quantum/Quantum/ makes a separate realm, it only shows the incapability of the CS in the Quantum field.

"*Bhagavan, please explain what characterizes false projections. How do false projections arise? What constitutes a false projection? And where are false projections found?*"

The Buddha told Mahamati, "Projections arise when there is attachment to the misperception of different objects. Mahamati, because people are unaware that their attachments to projections of what they grasp and of the one who grasps are nothing but perceptions of their own Minds, they fall prey to views of existence and nonexistence in which they are abetted by the views of followers of other paths and the habit-energy of their projections. And as they become attached to different external objects, the Mind, and what belongs to the Mind give rise to the projection of a self and what belongs to a self."

……

Mahamati:Why on the one hand, Bhagavan, does attachment to the discrimination of the existence of an unreal object give rise to projections and on the other hand attachment to ultimate truth not give rise to projections? ….

The Buddha said, "Because projections of ('true') existence or nonexistence do not arise. Projections do not arise when the external objects that appear as existing or not existing are seen to be nothing but perceptions of one's own Mind. By becoming aware that their projections are nothing but Mind. Thus, do they transform their body and Mind and finally see clearly all the stages and realms of self-Awareness of tathagatas and transcend views and projections regarding the five dharmas and modes of reality. This is why I say that projections arise from the attachment to things that are unreal and that once someone knows what is real they free themselves from the various projections of their own Mind."

This means that the foolish person does not see the earthly scene as a projection of a prejudice of the false ego because the Mind (represented by the false ego) has already had a prejudice.

Therefore, Nirvana is not EM but very close to EM and can be considered as real or non-illusional: When hearing that Heaven has a moon or stars, do not think of the moon or stars as seen in the PW. It should be considered that the moon and stars in Nirvana are much brighter than in PW and much more delicate. The physical or sensory organs cannot identify them.

The Buddha said to A Nan, "Have you ever heard that EM is perishable?

Therefore, the Nirvana (Mahayana) or Nibbana (Theravada), although not EM but close to should be both real as EM and is associated with space and time but not space and time as conceived in the Duality realm

For Theravada: Nibbana is to extinguish passion. And it also means Nir: out, the Vanna: the forest, that is, out of the dark forest, the troubled forest."

> *"Here is this land here, there is no land, there is no water, there is no fire, there is no wind, there is no emptiness, there is no limit... there is no wonderland; there is no this world, there is no future; there are no two moons. Here are the billions! I declare no coming, no going, no shelter, no destruction, no birth, no refuge, no transfer, no favor. This is the end of pain."*
> (Definition, UD 80-381)

The table is a witness. The table is the ultimate happiness of a spiritual object (vatthudhamma) that proves that the table is not a state of nothingness. The Buddha has described NB as "Infinite" (Anuttara), "Exceeding Outside" (Pariya), "Infinite Basic Place" (Paràyana), "Complete" (Tana), "Happy" (Siva), "First" (Kevala), "Immortal" (Akkhara), "Infinite in Pure" (Visuddha), "Superworld" (Lokuttara), "Eternal" (Amata), "Relief" (Mutti) etc...
In Udana and Itivuttka, the Buddha mentions the table as follows:
"See, there is an unborn (ajata), uninitiated (abhuta), unconstructed (akata) and unsubstituted (asamkara) state.

For Thervada Buddhism, Nirvana is a realm of stillness and homogeinity, for Mahayana considers it to be realm of working for salvation of living sentients without being disturbed by the worldly inversions,

(Phật tự thuyết, UD 80 - 381)

Where is Nirvana then?
- Nirvana is very close to EM; uniform, not coming, not going, somewhere or here is the same. Therefore, it is not wrong to say that Niirvana is in MW, egoless and devoid of Greed, Anger, and Ignorance

So, Nirvana is a real or actual entity and is a system consisting of:
- Nirvana without remainder Anupadisesa Nibbana Dhatu (devoid of Form and emotion Greed Ange Ignorance)
- Nirvana with remainder Sopadhi-zewa-nirvàịa, the Mind, and the body still remain in the PW (case Arahat)

According to Theravada, the Mind is free of the three poisons and detachable from the brain.
For Mahayana: the case of Buddha on the earthly world
(Transformative body Nirmanakaya and responding body Sambhogakaya

B. HEAVEN.
Heaven is a state of MW, often mentioned in the Bible, and is difficult to imagine. Conceiving that Heaven is a bright sky with a moon and a sun, as the world knows, is probably a big mistake because the earthly world sentients do not know the MW, and it isn't easy to express it through words. The Heavens where the moon, the star, and the sun ... described in the Bible belong to the unseen MW by the worldly people. The highest place of Heaven is God's residence (Kings 8:43, *the Lord in Heaven, the Lord's residence*). Angels are faithful to God; Churches can be in different Heavens. This means that Heaven is not a uniform world but has multiple levels. Therefore, Lucifer, the Angel, rebels with the war on Heaven (Satan) and the other angels against God to cause Heaven's war cannot share the same space with God. Similarly, as described in Psalms 30:19, the view of Heaven is not identical and close to EM. Heaven "consists of many levels of Heaven as described in Psalm 89:5: "O Lord, the Heavens will praise your wonders; your faith will also be praised in the congregation of the saints."

In summary, Nirvana, or the highest level of Paradise, is where no Greed, Anger, and ignorance can cause no war or chaos. Below Nirvana, or the highest level of Heaven, are Heavens with Paradise Wars, similar to Buddhist Worlds with the Form realm and high levels of Passion realm.

NON- DUALIISTIC PATHWAY
Nirvana, or the Highest level of Paradise, belongs to the Primordial World of Duality. Emptiness is the absolute Oneness that cannot be imagined or expressed in words. On the contrary, the Dualistic World is illusional and impermanent and can be easily expressed in words and easily imagined. So the same concept of the Middle Way / Mūla-Madhyamaka-kārikā of Bodhisattva Nagarjuna as centrality is not attached to Emptiness or Formlessness. Buddha, Bodhisatsava, and Arahats categorically represent three levels of the Nirvana and the Non-Dualistic concept of Masters and dimensions of the Nirvana simultaneously in both levels of oneness and Duality with no attachment to either entity. For example, Bodhisatsava helps people in the Earthly world but is not associated with earthly manifestation, as evidenced by the egolessness. All Happiness and sorrow need to be conceived like this: do not cling to Affliction since Affliction is Bodhi/Salvation, and do not cling to Happiness because of the impermanence. Similarly, in Meditation, Mind stillness is necessary for contemplation. However, contemplation will eventually decrease the Mind's stillness, and overriding stillness leads to the state of neither thinking nor not thinking as of a piece of wood or stone. There is no more Mind stillness or Contemplation in Omniscience when full Enlightenment is attained.

Chapter VI:
THE PHYSICAL WORLD IS THE PATH OF PERFECTION BY RE- EDUCATION TO ATTAIN HAPPINESS AND ULTIMAT TRUTH.

Summary

In the present world, the common notion is that the Buddha saves people from suffering so that this world is Heaven and human's true home. Though the Lord is all-powerful and compassionate, why can't He make the world a better place without war or famine? Despite the many prayers, suffering, as well as natural disasters, are increasing.

In Christianity, after human ancestors were expelled from Eden for their sins, their children continued to sin. He finally sent Jesus, his son, and representative of the Holy Spirit, to remind people of the Ten Commandments of God; the Lord Jesus has done many miracles of salvation, but the main purpose of the Lord is to go down to Earth to make hielj known, then to remind people to learn to love, to be good and to make no mistakes themselves. That is why the apostles of the Lord say that the Lord forgives sin for man. So, in this world, obstacles, and suffering are all set up by the Lord for man to learn to reform rather than punish sinners.

Buddhism, through its Noble Four Truths, teaches us to understand suffering as a means of reform. As Muhammad once said, "This world is a prison for those who have faith and Heaven for those who have no faith." The pleasures of this world are there to momentarily entertain us after learning but also to remind us of the true nature of pleasure in MW. After repentance cleanses sin, the veil of Ignorance is gradually lifted, revealing Nirvana, the realm of eternal bliss. This process of learning and reform, guided by our faith, should give us hope and motivation in our spiritual journey.

When human beings are good, then it is worthy and appropriate to live in Heaven or the Table as the original, as creatures have never made mistakes. Death is often regarded as the most significant suffering for those with many sins which need to continue to be repaired or to reset the cycle of learning and for those with no sins to be returned to an eternal home.

Because the Creation has many differences, there is also a choice for those who do not suffer to live in the blissful world. In the Western World of Amitabha or the Christian Paradise, those who believe in the Buddha or Jesus can also be born there after death, even though there is still much Karma. However, they are not suitable for the pure to live in the high-level Blissful Western world of Amitabha or in the high level of Paradise. Though born in the world of MW, they still need to learn to cultivate morality as in PW. Learning in this world of MW for those who sinned will last longer because of the lack of determination and the favorable environment for learning.

In summary, the visible world of about 5% of the Universe, which Buddhism often perceives as the world of suffering, where Buddha Sukkiyama is a supreme teacher, is a part of the Creation made for temporarily sheltering the sinners who need to learn to reform. Thus, the world of the Earth is an insignificant part of the Universe. Sentients in the MW know all the people of this world, but people in PM do not know much about what going on in the MW.

I. THE VISIBLE WORLD/PHYSICAL WORLD
The PW is about 5% of the Universe, and the Earthly world is an insignificant part of the Universe. As previously discussed, the visible world has many hindrances and suffering mixed with pleasure (eating, drinking, entertainment...) and temporary happiness. Everlasting happiness is impossible in this world, so everyone in the world wishes for permanent happiness.

Paradox in Philosophy and Religions about affliction and happiness.
The general notion of religion is that religion can save people from affliction and depression. All religions proclaim that the Supreme Lord has infinite love and compassion, loving all beings because they are His children. His love is greater than the ocean. Buddhism preaches that religion is to save suffering. The apostles of Jesus said that he sacrificed on the cross to redeem the sins of the creatures. Primitive sin is the root of human sin today. Buddhism is salvation. But for 2,500 years, man has continuously practiced salvation praying according to the Buddha's teachings through the Buddhist leaders. Human suffering continues, and suffering does not decrease but increases with time.

Why is it? People must have misunderstood the meaning of life in this world, misunderstood the essence of the spiritual teaching in major religions, followed phenomenal teaching, misunderstood the teachings of the Bible, sayings of Buddha, as well as the leaders of other great religions.

II. WHY IS THERE THE VISIBLE/PHYSICAL WORLD.
A. CHRISTANITY.
1. Adam and Eve committed a mistake and were driven out to Eden. The wrong man was vigilant, lest Grandpa come back to eat the fruit of life. They no longer live eternally like God. God does this not out of hatred, nor do parents today punish their children so that they learn to correct bad behavior. The Garden of Eden is the place of eternal happiness. Humans on this earth are descendants of the upper family.

Here is St. John's description of the city of Jerusalem built in the superworld after the destruction of sinful Babylon.

> *Revelation 21:9-21*
> ***The New Jerusalem, the Bride of the Lamb***
> ⁹ *One of the seven angels who had the seven bowls full of the seven last plagues came and said to me, "Come, I will show you the bride, the wife of the Lamb." ¹⁰ And he carried me away in the Spirit to a mountain great and high, and showed me the Holy City, Jerusalem, coming down out of Heaven from God. ¹¹ It shone with the glory of God, and its brilliance was like that of a very precious jewel, like a jasper, clear as crystal. ¹² It had a great, high wall with twelve gates, and with twelve angels at the gates. On the gates were written the names of the twelve tribes of Israel. ¹³ There were three gates on the east, three on the north, three on the south and three on the west. ¹⁴ The wall of the city had twelve foundations, and on them were the names of the twelve apostles of the Lamb.*
> ¹⁵ *The angel who talked with me had a measuring rod of gold to measure the city, its gates and its walls. ¹⁶ The city was laid out like a square, as long as it was wide. He measured the city with the rod and found it to be 12,000 stadia [a] in length, and as wide and high as it is long. ¹⁷ The angel measured the wall using human measurement, and it was 144 cubits [b] thick. [c] ¹⁸ The wall was made of jasper, and the city of pure gold, as pure as glass. ¹⁹ The foundations of the city walls were decorated with every kind of precious stone. The first foundation was jasper, the second sapphire, the third agate, the fourth emerald, ²⁰ the fifth onyx, the sixth ruby, the seventh chrysolite, the eighth beryl, the ninth topaz, the tenth turquoise, the eleventh jacinth, and the twelfth amethyst. [d] ²¹ The twelve gates were twelve pearls, each gate made of a single pearl. The great street of the city was of gold, as pure as transparent glass.*

2. Genesis 10:32

³² These are the clans of Noah's sons, according to their lines of descent, within their nations. From these the nations spread out over the earth after the flood....

The suffering is evident with all Christians, as well as of all mankind, in every time and place. This has also been explained in the above sections, which show that God, the Lord, has set up to teach and train humans for future living in conformity with Heaven. If that is a punishment, then the punishment does not come from hatred but from God's love, as He once sought to save them, the Adam and Eve family, from being heirless because there are people like Seth who believe in God and God's love, but they need to be re-educated. But the offspring of this family still committed so many sins.

Every training institution in the world needs labor to learn. Of course, students who do not study, enjoy too much pleasure, and do not graduate must stay in class or even be degraded and blamed.

---

1 Peter1:4-7

> *4 and into an inheritance that can never perish, spoil or fade. This inheritance is kept in Heaven for you, 5 who through faith are shielded by God's power until the coming of the salvation that is ready to be revealed in the last time. 6 In all this you greatly rejoice, though now for a little while you may have had to suffer grief in all kinds of trials. 7 These have come so that the proven genuineness of your faith—of greater worth than gold, which perishes even though refined by fire—may result in praise, glory and honor when Jesus Christ is revealed.*

God embodies Himself as Jesus to emulate His Son about Him to live moral life away from sin, that is to save man.

Matthew1:21

21 She will give birth to a son, and you are to give him the name Jesus, because he will save his people from their sins.".

Khải thị của St John viết: *"6 Đấng yêu thương chúng ta, đã lấy huyết mình rửa sạch tội lỗi chúng ta, và làm cho chúng ta nên nước Ngài". It is necessary to be described as a statue for man to learn sacrifice through which to baptize himself. That is because if he himself does not baptize himself for sin as the majority of mankind breaks the limit of ten teeth, then sin remains as full as it is today. So, the fact that God baptizes us for sin is conditional. The thing is that we must follow the example of the sufferer to baptize for illumination.*

Matthew 22:35-46

35 Có một thầy dạy luật trong bọn họ hỏi câu nầy để thử Ngài: 36 Thưa thầy, trong luật pháp, điều răn nào là lớn hơn hết? 37 Đức Chúa Jêsus đáp rằng: Ngươi hãy hết lòng, hết linh hồn, hết ý mà yêu mến Chúa, là Đức Chúa Trời ngươi. 38 Ấy là điều răn thứ nhất và lớn hơn hết. 39 Còn điều răn thứ hai đây, cũng như vậy: Ngươi hãy yêu kẻ lân cận như mình. 40 Hết thảy luật pháp và lời tiên tri đều bởi hai điều răn đó mà ra.

3. JUDGMENT.
 The Bible writes before the second return of God. Jesus Christ will judge those who are in this world for their lives in the world.

Ecclesiastes 12:13-14
New International Version
13 Now all has been heard; here is the conclusion of the matter: Fear God and keep his commandments, for this is the duty of all mankind. 14 For God will bring every deed into judgment, including every hidden thing, whether it is good or evil.

Matthew 25:46
46 It will be good for that servant whose master finds him doing so when he returns.
Peter 1:6-7
6 In this you rejoice, though now for a little while, if necessary, you have been grieved by various trials, 7 so that the tested genuineness of your faith—more precious than gold that perishes though it is tested by fire—may be found to result in praise and glory and honor at the revelation of Jesus Christ.
Revelation 22:11
He that is unjust, let him be unjust still: and he which is filthy, let him be filthy still: and he that is righteous, let him be righteous still

St John 14:1-3
[1] "Let not your hearts be troubled; believe in God, believe also in me. [2] In my Father's house are many rooms; if it were not so, would I have told you that I go to prepare a place for

you? [3] And when I go and prepare a place for you, I will come again and will take you to myself, that where I am you may be also.

Heaven/the metaphysical realm is a magnificent, magnificent place to be seen when St. John is introduced to the realm of Heaven through an angel with the error of Jesus and is asked to recapture to spread to the earthly. The propagation is expressed through seven letters to the seven churches in the Sub-A.

The event occurred when St. John, when imprisoned for preaching the Torah, finally gave the Holy Teeth to the reader to believe in the Torah and was not reduced.

Revelation 1:10, On the day of the Lord, I was inspired by the Holy Spirit, and there was a cry behind me, like a loud voice, 11 saying, What you see, write it down in a book and send it to the seven churches.
....
Revelation 22:18-18 I tell anyone who hears the prophecy in this book: If anyone adds anything to this prophecy, God will add to him the evil that is written in this book. 19 And whoever shall take away any of the words of this prophetic book, God will take away his share of the tree of life and of the holy city, which are written in this book.

Revelation 1:1-20
The Revelation of Jesus Christ, which God gave Him to show His servants—things which must shortly take place. And He sent and signified it by His angel to His servant John, who bore witness to the word of God, and to the testimony of Jesus Christ, to all things that he saw. Blessed is he who reads and those who hear the words of this prophecy, and keep those things which are written in it; for the time is near. John, to the seven churches which are in Asia: Grace to you and peace from Him who is and who was and who is to come, and from the seven Spirits who are before His throne, and from Jesus Christ, the faithful witness, the firstborn from the dead, and the ruler over the kings of the earth. To Him who loved us and washed us from our sins in His own blood, and has made us kings and priests to His God and Father, to Him be glory and dominion forever and ever. Amen. Behold, He is coming with clouds, and every eye will see Him, even they who pierced Him. And all the tribes of the earth will mourn because of Him. Even so, Amen. "I am the Alpha and the Omega, the Beginning and the End," says the Lord, "who is and who was and who is to come, the Almighty." I, John, both your brother and companion in the tribulation and kingdom and patience of Jesus Christ, was on the island that is called Patmos for the word of God and for the testimony of Jesus Christ. I was in the Spirit on the Lord's Day, and I heard behind me a loud voice, as of a trumpet, saying, "I am the Alpha and the Omega, the First and the Last," and, "What you see, write in a book and send it to the seven churches which are in Asia: to Ephesus, to Smyrna, to Pergamos, to Thyatira, to Sardis, to Philadelphia, and to Laodicea." Then I turned to see the voice that spoke with me. And having turned I saw seven golden lampstands, and in the midst of the seven lampstands One like the Son of Man, clothed with a garment down to the feet and girded about the chest with a golden band. His head and hair were white like wool, as white as snow, and His eyes like a flame of fire; His feet were like fine brass, as if refined in a furnace, and His voice as the sound of many waters; He had in His right hand seven stars, out of His mouth went a sharp two-edged sword, and His countenance was like the sun shining in its strength. And when I saw Him, I fell at His feet as dead. But He laid His right hand on me, saying to me, "Do not be afraid; I am the First and the Last. I am He who lives, and was dead, and behold, I am alive forevermore. Amen. And I have the keys of Hades and of Death. Write the things which you have seen, and the things which are, and the things which will take place after this. The mystery of the seven stars which you saw in My right hand, and the seven golden lampstands: The seven stars are the angels of the seven churches, and the seven lampstands which you saw are the seven churches.

Then St. John draws described the MW in the Heaven:

> *Throne in Heaven*
> **Chapter 4**
> 4 *After this I looked, and there before me was a door standing open in Heaven. And the voice I had first heard speaking to me like a trumpet said, "Come up here, and I will show you what must take place after this." ² At once I was in the Spirit, and there before me was a throne in Heaven with someone sitting on it. ³ And the one who sat there had the appearance of jasper and ruby. A rainbow that shone like an emerald encircled the throne. ⁴ Surrounding the throne were twenty-four other thrones, and seated on them were twenty-four elders. They were dressed in white and had crowns of gold on their heads. ⁵ From the throne came flashes of lightning, rumblings and peals of thunder. In front of the throne, seven lamps were blazing. These are the seven spirits [a] of God. ⁶ Also in front of the throne there was what looked like a sea of glass, clear as crystal.*
> *In the center, around the throne, were four living creatures, and they were covered with eyes, in front and in back. ⁷ The first living creature was like a lion, the second was like an ox, the third had a face like a man, the fourth was like a flying eagle. ⁸ Each of the four living creatures had six wings and was covered with eyes all around, even under its wings. Day and night they never stop saying:*
> *"'Holy, holy, holy*
> *is the Lord God Almighty,' [b]*
> *who was, and is, and is to come."*
> *⁹ Whenever the living creatures give glory, honor and thanks to him who sits on the throne and who lives for ever and ever, ¹⁰ the twenty-four elders fall down before him who sits on the throne and worship him who lives for ever and ever. They lay their crowns before the throne and say:*
> *¹¹ "You are worthy, our Lord and God, to receive glory and honor and power, for you created all things, and by your will they were created and have their being."*

St. John describes the punishment of the Babylonians.
Revelation 18:1-3 The angel announces the fall of Babylon
1 Then I saw another angel coming down from Heaven with great power, and his glory made the earth bright. 2 He cried with a loud voice, It has fallen, it has fallen, the great Babylon! It has become the horse of the devil, the horse of all unclean Gods, the horse of all unclean and disgusting birds, 3 for all nations have drunk the wine of its horrendous prostitution, the king of the earth has forged with it, and the merchants of the earth have become rich by its infinite luxury!"
The people of God must go away.

Leaving Eden Garden, Adam and Eve had to work hard so they would see their mistakes because in joy and happiness, there is no suffering, so they would not recognize their mistakes. Adam Eve's first child killed his younger brother Abel out of jealousy. Cain and his youngest son, Seth, continued to make many mistakes and crimes. God was very saddened to have created this kind of man, so he decided to remove them and remove them from the world.

He only retained the family of Noah, who had three sons and each pair of animals.

> *Genesis 6:5 says, "The Lord saw that the wickedness of man was great in the earth, and that every intention of the thoughts of his heart was only evil continually".This is why the sin comes from the ancestors. Successive crimes may be due to genetics and epigenetics (due to environmental influence on genes), education, family, and society. So, the sin of ancestry does not mean that children are punished because of ancestors' or parents' sins. In short, the Adam Eve family is a criminal.*

In summary, this world, and maybe the entire visible world, is not the home of humans. The sentient is sent here to learn to reform, suffer, repent, and correct the mistakes of his ancestors and his own. Jesus came down here for three years to remind people of God and the 10 Moses' commandments, especially commandments 1 and 2 loved to listen to God's word and love (love the neighborhood). During retraining and learning, temporary entertainment creates joy, such as temporarily forgetting the suffering in learning (and also introducing the happy joy in the MW) until graduates ascend to Heaven with eternal happiness in Heaven, which is the original home. So, the hindrances, suffering, afflictions, and even death are the lessons, not hatred or punishment. Humans who are stubborn and do not believe in Jesus will remain forever in this world in the Hell of long-lasting suffering until they awaken because they do not deserve to be in Heaven.**Marrhew 1:21**

<u>21</u> *Người sẽ sanh một trai, ngươi khá đặt tên là Jêsus, vì chính con trai ấy sẽ cứu dân mình ra khỏi tội.*

B. BUDDHISM
Bảng 1: Cấp bậc Hồn hay Cõi Luân Hồi và cõi Trời theo Phật giáo và Đạo giáo

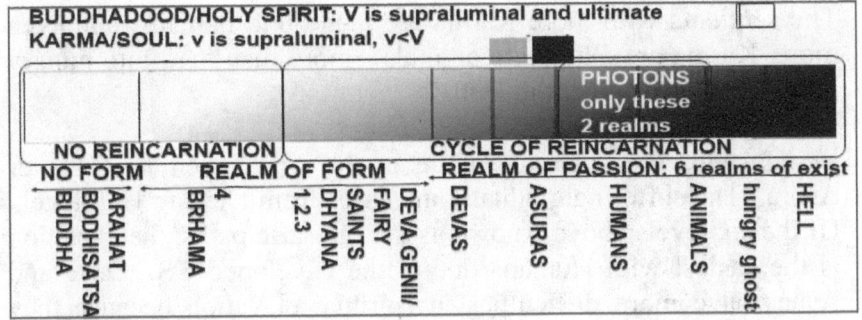

The Buddhist view is expressed by the conception of Three Realms, characterized by No Form, the Form, and the Passion Realms. In the Realm of Passion, Hell and hungry Ghost levels are devoid of Photons but are distinct from the metaphysical realm. The difference between the MW and Hell and hungry Ghost levels of the Passion Realms is the Karma in the Hell and hungry Ghost levels is too heavy and dense enough to obscure the Buddha's light (but cannot cover up all Buddha's light so that Buddha can see Hell and hungry Ghost levels). The characteristic of the PW is that Photons are present only in it.

This division is based on the purity of the spirit that is often defiled by Karma. Karma is made up of ignorance and evil deeds. Karma is an accident that occurs when Creation develops from EM.

When the intention or a Thought has occurred, EM is no longer as it is and changes; there will be no other EM because EM is unique. The idea is the intention of God to create the Universe. Buddhism does not say anything about the meaning of the Initial Thought, but Christianity says that the will of God created the Universe. The spiritual books write that man continues committing mistakes and sins so that God decides to erase humans from the earthly.:

Genesis 6:5-8:22
[5] *The LORD saw how great the wickedness of the human race had become on the earth, and that every inclination of the thoughts of the human heart was only evil all the time.* [6] *The LORD regretted that he had made human beings on the earth, and his heart was deeply troubled.* [7] *So the LORD said, "I will wipe from the face of the earth the human race I have created—and with them the animals, the birds and the creatures that move along the ground—for I regret that I have made them."* [8] *But Noah found favor in the eyes of the LORD......*

The sentients with more Karma are made into humans, and even more, Karma are made into animals—more than that, into hungry ghosts or imprisonment in Hell.

Beings with less Karma can be in the MW, such as Deva or Asura. The suffering gradually increases from Deva to Hell level. Of the six levels above, known as the samsaric paths, the elevation is the easiest with Humans due to the developed CS. Deva and Asuas have more difficulties in spiritual elevation because they endure little suffering, so it isn't easy to learn. Animals and hungry ghosts are also challenging to learn because they are most ignorant due to the thick veil of Ignorance with erroneous CS and heavy Karma.

III. THE WORLD OF HUMANS AND ANIMALS.
Unlike other worlds, the visible world recognizes things through the CS. CS is created from the brain. brain, as well as other objects in the visible world, are constructed based on Photons and related elementary particles.
What MW are made as elementary particles is entirely unknown by science or CS.

However, the MW has Dark Force and black matter of unknown nature.

A. THE PHYSICAL WORLD
1. PHOTONS (Fig 12)
Returning to the Universe, the celestial bodies galaxies are in the Universe and retain such position thanks to Newton's gravitational force. Einstein's General Relativity theory describes the Universe according to the time-space curvature caused by the gravity of a galaxy.

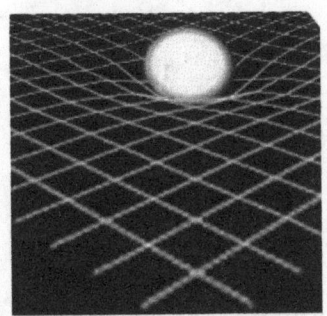
F12

The light with Photons, though not weighing, flows close to giant stars and is bent by prominent stars as they travel in the direction of space (H1.3). It is the phenomenon of gravitational lensing, similar to the phenomenon of refraction when we see the stick in the water as broken.

2. The four fundamental forces in physics and Dark Force142

Four forces create the Universe. Understanding these four forces, physicists can see, measure, and sense the material world of the Universe.
•   Weak Nuclear Force keeps the particles from being damaged, using particles w and z, weak at far range but strong at close range.
•   Strong Force connects the Quarks in the nucleus of an atom. This is the strongest force. The force in atomic bomb accounts for this force
•   Electromagnetic Force uses less powerful Photons, but the range of influence is indefinite.
•   Gravity is gravity (like the Earth's attraction force) using the graviton particle as the designated name, but it has not yet been found; it is even weaker but long-range.
•   Dark Force (not confirmed)
Dark Force was conceived when dark matter (23%), baryonic matter (4%), and Neutrinos (<1%) accounted for only 27% of the mass of the Universe. Again, the Universe is accelerating in expansion, which Einstein's General Theory equation cannot explain without the concept of Dark Force.

Grand Unified Theory GUT.

Of the scientifically confirmed forces, electromagnetic/electromagnetic force, weak force, and strong/strong force can originate from a single force in the GUT theory, which postulates the force at a very early time after BB.

Theory of Everything TOE
The Theory of Everything TOE combines these three forces and gravity.
The above idea is very reasonable on the principle that the Universe originated from EM is omnipotent (and omniscient) with unlimited power... from this unlimited power, develop five forces, namely Electromagnetic/electromagnetic force, Weak force, Strong force, gravity, and Dark Force.

3. THE SOUL.
As proposed in chapter I the Soul is composed of the:
    DM: belongs to MW.
    Neutrino: intermediate between MW and PW

When the Soul enters the brain, Neutrinos in the Soul are attached to an Electron and, therefore, have the electromagnetic properties to adhere to neuronal synapses.,

IV. THE METAPHYSICAL WORLD IS THE SOUL'S HOME LAND.
The MW has no Photons, visible matter, or weak or strong forces. But the MW has a DM that is associated with gravity and Dark Forces with unlimited strength and beyond Quantum particles, smaller the Photons. As a result, the structure and the quality in MW are much finer, more delicate, magnificent, and ingenious.

In the previous section on the Soul, the DM is the main constituent of the Soul.

In Buddhism's sutra P. Mahāpadāna Sutta, Long Discourse, the MW is also populated by beings of higher rank than humans, without Karma or less Karma (such as Arahat).

God and the saints in Christianity are all in the MW.

As previously presented, the structure of MW is very delicate, exceeding the threshold of Consciousness. Hence, the Creation and objects are overwhelmingly splendid, with magical fluorescence and fragrance of indescribable extent.
People in the visible world are misguided by ignorance, which reflects the CS.

V. THE PHYSICAL WORLD IS MADE FOR THE SINNERS
The Creation of matter and energy in the GUT Grand Unified Theory PW is to create a separate world for those who disobey the commandments of the GUT. People are sent down to this world from Heaven /the metaphysical world for reeducation. Many sinners who do not learn but seek every way to enjoy should consider this place Paradise. They have little chance of going to Heaven. The world is a prison for the believer and a paradise for the unbeliever. Prophet Muhammad 2956)

In the Bible, when Adam and Eve were expelled from the Garden of Eden, the Garden was carefully guarded not to let him or their offspring return (when not worthy). The respective things in this world are equipped with electromagnetic, weak, and strong forces, and the respective particles make beings in the PW completely blind to Heaven and MW. The GUT force and the elementary particles are the materials that make up visible matter (baryonic represents the veil of Ignorance that obliterates humans and animals and restricts them in the physical world. They must endure the suffering mixed with momentary pleasure to help them overcome hardship and learn. When successful, the veil of Ignorance is cleansed/removed to ascend to Heaven.
Therefore, the suffering through, hardship, illness and death are set up in the PW as a teaching tool for learning. The Creator will never remove until the last sinner who learns successfully reaches the level of Perfection.

SECOND THERMODYNAMIC LAW (TDL2): ENTROPY (NATURAL LAW OF DISTURBANCE)
1. The first law of thermal mechanics is about energy conservation: in a closed system, the energy supplied and the

energy produced, including the energy heating the system, are equal.

2. The second law is drawn from the universal and common sense of experience that heat always moves from the highest temperature down to the lowest temperature, and this process is natural to follow only one direction and cannot be reversed naturally. When a change in the temperature in the opposite direction is made, a pump is required. Doing so means increasing the disturbance of the two high-to-low systems and the surrounding environment due to the addition of the pump). This disorder is called Entropy (index of disturbance). *This is the principle of the Dualistic world that has lost the supersymmetry of Emptiness/EM. Because of asymmetry, events occur only in one direction, from High to Low, Strong to Weak*
TDL2 says as follows:
A closed system that does not exchange energy with the environment will have Entropy constantly increasing or unchanging over time.
Every transmission or transformation of energy increases the Entropy of the system.
In order for a process to happen spontaneously, it must increase the Entropy of the Universe.

For example, people are just getting older and can't be younger, or a room is getting dusty and can't be reversed. The Entropy represents the increasingly disruptive environment that can't stop. The other expression of this phenomenon is the *time arrow*.

When referring to time, one refers to the dualistic world or the PW (The Ultimate Realm/The Oneness World is EM that has no time or space).
Time makes the PW chaotic and messy (increased Entropy). Physicists are contemplative. Unfortunately, many people wish that time would make things better, which can only be seen in a short period of time, but long-term TDL2 indicates that the environment is worse. Knowing that TDL2 only applies to the Dualistic world and does not apply to the Oneness World of Paradise or Nirvana.

An example is the genetic coding system that constitutes the human body's DNA in the chromosomes, which is imperfect and causes too many diseases. The more damage the system does when humans get older, the more damage the system's DNA has. Although there is a repair mechanism, this mechanism fails in many cases. It is the cause of most cancers and other illnesses...

Entropy correlates with the two main components of Inversion/Fooliness (see page 33) caused by False Though. Entropy also represents the loss of the (Neither homogeneity Not Heterogeneity of the principle of Eight Negatives of Nagarujuna's Middle way. So entropy is a phenomenon of Unrest, which is essential, non-concessional in the PW.

Then, of course, the Physicists also point out that humans are increasingly suffering because the environment is increasingly troubled by natural disasters, accidents, wars, hatred, and lies, a less peaceful, loving, and reconciling environment. It is the process of EM (neither homogeneous nor Heterogenous) degenerating into a Dualistic realm with discrimination and contradiction. TDL1 and 2 are meaningfully made by God, for this PW.

When creating a human with a DNA system, it is clearly not perfect. God's omniscience and love are for sure to be able to do better, but He did not; the Bible says only for men to live 120 years. If the more perfect DNA system existed on Earth, humans could live 1000 years or more and not become ugly when getting old. Life expectancy up to 120 years is probably enough for humans to cultivate morality if it is difficult to learn.

So God created a world full of turmoil, entropy increasingly higher so that people learn to overcome moral hardships to become good (such as military school new recruits crossing warrior barriers, or interned students of disciplined private schools). Whoever wants to enjoy it stays in the classroom without graduation, not going to heaven, but must re-enter and learn more difficult tasks. Eternal happiness is impossible in this Physical world, for suffering and joy are always intertwined.

The problem is that people who are proud of themselves do not recognize their sins, so they do not consider the school of life as a school, but rather have a fun realm, complain about not having enough fun because life is too short, and do not know that the original home is in heaven. Muhammad said *"the world is a prison for those who believe in Allah and a paradise for those who do not"* The road back to heaven is difficult and opposed to life stream with only a few go, as St. Matthew said: (Matthew 7:13-14) Enter the narrow door, for the door is wide, and the door is open, and it leads to destruction, and there are many who enter. But narrow doors and narrow roads lead to life

The Four Noble Truth sutra is the Buddha's first passage in the proclamation of Dharma: if you don't know that life is the ocean of suffering to learn to destroy suffering, then you can't get rid of it.

Therefore, the difficulties of aging, sickness, aging, and death are raised by the Creator/God as a teaching tool for learning. In other words, the world of this physical word was given to sinned humans sent from Paradise to this world to learn to be transformed. God will never remove the hardships until the last sinner finally learns to reach Heavenly Goodness.

Jesus heals a man born blind:

John 9:1–5
9 *As he went along, he saw a man blind from birth. 2 His disciples asked him, "Rabbi,ᵖ who sinned,ᵠ this manᵉ or his parents,ˢ that he was born blind?"*   3 *"Neither this man nor his parents sinned," said* Jesus, *"but this happened so that the works of God might be displayed in him.ᵗ 4 As long as it is day,ᵘ we must do the works of him who sent me. Night is coming, when no one can work. 5 While I am in the world, I am the light of the world."ᵛ*

Jesus said the blindness did not come from the man or his parent's sin but was imposed by God (from the education and repair of the original mistakes)

As in the Lotus sutra, chapter 16 says:

Chapter XVII Description of Merits *Thereupon, when the great assembly heard the Buddha explain that his lifes span was of such a great number of kalpas, an immeasurable, limitless, incalculable number of sentient beings were greatly benefited.*

*Then the Bhagavat addressed Bodhisattva Mahāsattva Maitreya, saying: "O Ajita! When I explained the great length of this Tathāgata's lifespan, sentient beings, equal to the sands of the six hundred and eighty myriad of koṭis of nayutas of Ganges Rivers in number, gained understanding of the truth of the nonorigination of all dharmas. Furthermore, a thousand times this number of bodhisattvas mahāsattvas attained the power of recollecting what they hear; and bodhisattva mahāsattvas equal to the number of particles in one world attained unhindered eloquence. Moreover, there were bodhisattva mahāsattvas equal to the particles in one world who attained the power of tenacious memory which revolves hundreds of thousands of myriads of koṭis of immeasurable times. There were also bodhisattva mahāsattvas equal to the number of particles in **the great manifold cosmos** who turned the irreversible wheel of the Dharma, and bodhisattva mahāsattvas equal to the number of particles in two medium-sized manifold cosmos who turned the purified wheel of the Dharma. "Furthermore, there were bodhisattva mahāsattvas equal to the number of particles in one small-sized cosmos who will be able to attain highest, complete enlightenment after eight births; bodhisattva mahāsattvas equal to the number of particles in the four fourfold continents who will attain highest, complete enlightenment after four births; bodhisattva mahāsattvas equal to the number of particles in the threefold four continents who will attain highest, complete enlightenment after three births; bodhisattva mahāsattvas equal to the number of particles in the twofold four continents who will attain highest, complete enlightenment after two births; and bodhisattva mahāsattvas equal to the number of particles in the four continents who will attain highest, complete enlightenment after one birth. Moreover, there were sentient beings equal to the number of particles in the eightfold great manifold cosmos, in all of whom the thought of highest, complete enlightenment had awakened." When the Buddha explained that these bodhisattva mahāsattvas had attained deep insight into the Dharma, māndārava and great māndārava flowers rained down from the sky, scattering over the Buddhas who were seated on lion seats under immeasurable hundreds of thousands of myriads of koṭis of jeweled trees; and they scattered over Śākyamuni Buddha and the Tathāgata Prabhūtaratna, who had attained parinirvāṇa long ago, both of whom were sitting on the lion seat in a seven-jeweled stupa; they also scattered over all of the great bodhisattvas and the fourfold assembly. Finely powdered sandalwood and aloeswood incense also rained down, and Heavenly drums resounded in the sky with a deep and beautiful sound. One thousand kinds of Heavenly garments, draped with strings of pearl, jewels, and wish-fulfilling gems (maṇi), rained down, filling the nine directions. Priceless incense burned in various jeweled incense holders, and its fragrance spread spontaneously throughout the great assembly as an offering. Above each Buddha there were bodhisattvas holding banners and umbrellas that extended upward to the Brahma world. These bodhisattvas praised the Buddhas by singing immeasurable verses with beautiful voices. "Why is this? Because the Tathāgata perceives all the marks of the tripleworld as they really are: **that there is no birth and death, coming or going**; that there is also no existence or extinction in the world, truth or falsehood, sameness or difference. The Tathāgata does not view the triple world as sentient beings in the triple world see it. **The Tathāgata perceives such things clearly and without mistakes.** "Since sentient beings have various natures, desires, behaviors, thoughts, and distinctions, the Tathāgata, **wanting to cause them to plant roots of good** merit, has explained various teachings through a variety of examples, explanations, and illustrations. He has not desisted from doing Buddha acts even for a single moment and in this way, it has been an extremely long time since I attained Buddhahood. My lifespan is immeasurable and incalculable. I abide **forever without entering parinirvāṇa**. "O sons of a virtuous family! The lifespan that I first attained through practicing the bodhisattva path has not yet expired. It is twice as great as the number previously mentioned. Although I do not actually enter parinirvāṇa I proclaim that I do. It is through this skillful means that the Tathāgata leads and inspires sentient beings. "**Why is this? Because if the Buddha abides a long time in this world, those who have few qualities do not plant roots of good merit, acquire poor and superficial characters, are attached to the desires of the five senses**, and enter into the web of illusions and false views. If they see the Tathāgata always existing without extinction, they then become proud, self-willed, and negligent. The thought that the Buddha is difficult to meet and that he is to be respected cannot awaken in them. That is why the Tathāgata teaches through skillful means, saying: **O monks! You should know that the appearance of the Buddhas in the world is very difficult to encounter.** "Why is this? Because* *some of those with little merit may not see the Buddha during the passage of immeasurable hundreds of thousands of myriads of koṭis of kalpas. "For this reason, I say: O monks! It is difficult to meet the Tathāgata. "Hearing such words, the thought that it is very difficult to meet the Tathāgata will certainly awaken in these sentient beings. Longing and yearning for the Buddha, they will plant roots of good merit. For this reason, although the Tathāgata does not really pass into extinction, he nevertheless says he does. "Furthermore, O sons of a virtuous family, the teaching of all the BuddhaTathāgatas is exactly like this. It is entirely true, never false, all for the sake of saving sentient beings. "Suppose there were an excellent doctor. He is wise, knowledgeable, his prescriptions are effective, and he has skillfully cured a variety of diseases. This man has many sons, say ten, twenty, or even one hundred in number. For some reason, he has to go far off to another country and, while he is away, his children, whom he has left behind, drink some poison. The poison starts to take effect and they roll on the ground in agony. "At this moment their father returns home. Some of the children who have taken the poison are delirious, while others are not. Seeing their father in the distance they all rejoice greatly and kneeling respectfully address him, saying: It is good that you have returned safely. In our ignorance we took this poison by mistake. We entreat you to cure and save us, and restore us to life. "Seeing his children suffering in this way, the father searches for benefi- cial herbs possessed of good color, aroma, and flavor, according to the medical manual. Blending them together after grinding and sifting, he gives the mixture to the children and says: This is an extremely beneficial medicine with good color, aroma, and flavor. All of you take it! It will quickly remove your pain and you will never be afflicted again. "Then the **children who have not become delirious see this beneficial medicine of good color and aroma, and immediately take it. The affliction s completely removed and they are cured. The remaining children, those who are delirious, seeing their father coming to them,** rejoice and ask him to seek a cure for their illness. Although he offers them the medicine, they will not take it. Why is this? Why is this? The poison has so deeply penetrated them that they have become delirious. They do not think that the medicine with good color and aroma is good. "The father thinks: These children are to be pitied. The poison has completely warped their Minds. Although they rejoiced upon seeing me and sought a cure they will not take this beneficial medicine. I will now cause them to take this medicine through skillful means. "Then he says to them: You should know that I am now old and feeble, close to death. I will now leave this beneficial medicine here. You should take it. Do not worry about not recovering. "Having left these instructions, he goes to another country and sends a messenger back home to tell them: 'Your father has already died.' Upon hearing that their father is dead, the children become very distressed and think: If our father had lived he would have taken pity on us and protected us. But now, abandoning us, he has died in a distant country. "They now consider themselves orphans having no one to rely upon. Through constant grieving their Minds become clear, and only then do they realize that the medicine has fine color, aroma, and flavor. They immediately take it and the poison is completely driven out. The father, hearing that all his children have completely recovered, immediately returns and makes his appearance." The Buddha then asked the bodhisattvas: "O sons of a virtuous family! Do you think there is anyone who would say that this good doctor is guilty of lying?" The bodhisattvas replied: "No, we do not, O Bhagavat!" The Buddha said: "I am just like this. Since I became a Buddha, immeasurable, limitless, hundreds of thousands of myriads of koṭis of nayutas of incalculable kalpas have passed. Though for the sake of sentient beings, I use skillful means and say that I will enter parinirvāṇa, there is no one who could rightly say that I am guilty of falsehood."*

Meaning: The Three Realms develop from the EM that is permanent and is not associated with birth or death. But after Creation, there is a world of passion associated with birth and death. Buddha attained the Buddhahood level in innumerable eons. Buddha did not stay long in the PW, where humans can get bored and do not appreciate, therefore making himself difficult to find.

Or even pretends to die. On hearing the death, humans start appreciating Buddha's teaching. This is not called a lie.

Listening to understanding and repeating the sutra to understand MW is a great merit.

The story of the blind turtle and a piece of wood on the sea in the book of A Ham/Nikaya indicates the difficulty of meeting the Buddha during the French times. Since the day that people were brought down to the world of My Mother to learn to reform, many have returned to their homes in the land of Nest. It is that they have fewer mistakes; the later, the fewer people are educated, the more people who remain make mistakes, the denser the membrane of ignorance because the advances of technical science are the factors that contributed to the degeneratice Dharma in this era. Thus, it is harder to meet the Buddha before because of this ignorance membrane;

The blind turtle.
  Buddha told the teachers that: "This land has become a sea. Then there was a blind turtle that lived countless times, after hundreds of thousands of years, but not once. At the sea there is a tree floating, when the east, when the west because of the waves of the wind. There is only one hole in the tree. But is it easy for the blind turtle to look for a tree and get his head in the tree?"

  A Nan responded that: "White world! It is difficult to find it because the turtle is blind, the East Sea is too large, the tree floats again, moves along the waves of the wind, the four directions of the East and West are going to park somewhere, so it is definitely difficult to find it."

  Buddha teaches: "The blind turtle, the tree that is hard to find, but there is hope, not come like a foolish man, floating in five animals and rebirthing a human body is more difficult than the turtle to meet the tree trunk several times. Therefore, you must improve today, seeking all means to develop your desire to learn more and more.

Lotus Sutra Chapter XVII
Description of Merits
Thereupon, when the great assembly heard the Buddha explain that his lifes span was of such a great number of kalpas, an immeasurable, limitless, incalculable number of sentient beings were greatly benefited.
Then the Bhagavat addressed Bodhisattva Mahāsattva Maitreya, saying: "O Ajita! When I explained the great length of this Tathāgata's lifespan, sentient beings, equal to the sands of the six hundred and eighty myriad of koṭis of nayutas of Ganges Rivers in number, gained understanding of the truth of the nonorigination of all dharmas. Furthermore, a thousand times this number of bodhisattvas mahāsattvas attained the power of recollecting what they hear; and bodhisattva mahāsattvas equal to the number of particles in one world attained unhindered eloquence. Moreover, there were bodhisattva mahāsattvas equal to the particles in one world who attained the power of tenacious memory which revolves hundreds of thousands of myriads of koṭis of immeasurable times. There were also bodhisattva mahāsattvas equal to the number of

> *particles in the great manifold cosmos who turned the irreversible wheel of the Dharma, and bodhisattva mahāsattvas equal to the number of particles in two medium-sized manifold cosmos who turned the purified wheel of the Dharma.*
>
> *"Furthermore, there were bodhisattva mahāsattvas equal to the number of particles in one small-sized cosmos who will be able to attain highest, complete enlightenment after eight births; bodhisattva mahāsattvas equal to the number of particles in the four fourfold continents who will attain highest, complete enlightenment after four births; bodhisattva mahāsattvas equal to the number of particles in the threefold four continents who will attain highest, complete enlightenment after three births; bodhisattva mahāsattvas equal to the number of particles in the twofold four continents who will attain highest, complete enlightenment after two births; and bodhisattva mahāsattvas equal to the number of particles in the four continents who will attain highest, complete enlightenment after one birth. Moreover, there were sentient beings equal to the number of particles in the eightfold great manifold cosmos, in all of whom the thought of highest, complete enlightenment had awakened."*
>
> *When the Buddha explained that these bodhisattva mahāsattvas had attained deep insight into the Dharma, māndārava and great māndārava flowers rained down from the sky, scattering over the Buddhas who were seated on lion seats under immeasurable hundreds of thousands of myriads of koṭis of jeweled trees; and they scattered over Śākyamuni Buddha and the Tathāgata Prabhūtaratna, who had attained parinirvāṇa long ago, both of whom were sitting on the lion seat in a seven-jeweled stupa; they also scattered over all of the great bodhisattvas and the fourfold assembly. Finely powdered sandalwood and aloeswood incense also rained down, and Heavenly drums resounded in the sky with a deep and beautiful sound. One thousand kinds of Heavenly garments, draped with strings of pearl, jewels, and wish-fulfilling gems (maṇi), rained down, filling the nine directions. Priceless incense burned in various jeweled incense holders, and its fragrance spread spontaneously throughout the great assembly as an offering. Above each Buddha there were bodhisattvas holding banners and umbrellas that extended upward to the Brahma world. These bodhisattvas praised the Buddhas by singing immeasurable verses with beautiful voices.*

This means that Buddha has a very long life as Buddha, and incalculable number of Bodhisatsava have countless Dharma disciplines and disciples.

In summary, meeting Buddha or knowing the sutras is precious but is never distractive in the cultivation. Similarly, ascending to Heaven, the spiritual realm, and the Pure Western Land aided by the Divine Power of Buddha is only the first stage of learning to reform. The Amitaba's Western Pure Land has no literal suffering, no Hell, and it is harder to practice than in the earthly world, which has many tools to cultivate Mind. Tao is non-discriminative; the Mind's merit deserves to which position it is, therefore.

For example, the Amitaba's western Pure Land is divided into nine levels composed of three sublevels of each High, Middle and Low levels.

Being at the Low Low level has to stay in the rooy of Lotus Tree for even 12 eons, much longer than being in Hell.

For Beings in the spiritual realms below Arahat level, it is still difficult to learn because there is no suffering or little suffering, and no human body.

Praying without practicing is hard to imagine, achieving the desired result of happiness in the world of morality. Practice correctly and understand the dharma, the morality Egolessness, the Four immeasurable Minds of Virtue, the Eightfold Path of Dharmma, is the hardest but shortest path to return to the homeland of Nirvana

Helping the suffering person belongs to the Four Immeasurable Minds of Virtue, but because suffering is the bitter medicine to overcome hardship and not to remove hindrances. For example, Antibiotics may be used to treat the infection, but infectious agents remain forever in the world.

Similarly, technical advancement of science for humans to overcome suffering. Momentary pleasure is useful as a springboard to facilitate endurance and continuing learning and is not for excessive fun.

Death is often regarded as the most significant suffering for those with many sins, which need to continue to be repaired or to reset the cycle of learning, and for those with no sins to be returned to an eternal home. This latter case is often associated with natural death without much suffering and planning

Ascetism in Buddhism
Ascetism is one of the Buddhist methods of cultivation in enduring suffering. Give up money and fame. Mendicant monk Minh Tue has said, "I, a Buddhist son, am going to pray for liberation." The ascetic monk accepts difficulties in eating, wearing, and living.
- Cultivating virtue, developing the wisdom.
- Purifying three Karmas of body, speech and thought

According to Theravada Buddhism, asceticism has 13 practices:
1. *wearing clothes made up of discarded pieces.*
2. *having three robes.*
3. *eating given food.*
4. *mendicant at successive house.*
5. *eating after sitting once a day*
6. *eating in a bowl.*
7. *no receiving excess food*
8. *live in the woods.*
9. *living under the tree.*
10. *living outdoor.*
11. *living at the cemetery.*
12. *living anywhere.*
13. *sleeping while sitting*

The above practices are not prescribed by the Buddha. Buddha himself was almost dying and advised the "Middle way" by avoiding the two extremes that are miserable and joyful to achieve fruitful morality.

The meaning:
- The determination, also known as the effort, is one of the Eightfold Noble Truths of Buddhist cultivation. The determination, also referred to as "Bodhi" (liberation), is the key and determining factor for the success of the spiritual practice.
- Renunciation: the Buddha leaves the status of a prince and owns nothing. Cultivation is to get rid of unnecessary belongings and not add something because man is born from the Creator (ST), so as the image of God (God created man in His image), but mistakenly being attached with Karmas (money, family, and inversions of society, ...) When the Karma is cleansed, only Buddhahood remains, i.e. . Renunciation is also one of the Noble Eightfold Paths of morality, which is egolessness.
- Egolessness is the hallmark of Buddhism. Not seen in other religions. Egolessness is one of the Noble Eightfold Truths. All things are born from God (or God, the Creator), the Father of all species, regardless of status or title, so all things are invisible and have no self or possession of

anything except the right to life that God gives. Therefore, only God is Father, and all is Son.
Acetism itself does not create the Mindfulness or Omniscience, but generates many benefits.

Acetism in Christianity.
John the Baptist was the first person to practice asceticism. Then, the Christian Council converted the asceticism from abandoning the wilderness and returning to the service of the poor and sick, returning to the poor spirit of the Gospel. In addition, asceticism means fasting and includes many other forms, such as caring for patients and leaving home to strange places on mission.

The concept includes
Prayer: Prayer hours are regulated according to the law.
Work is to sanctify oneself, to nurture oneself while helping the poor.
Life is hard with vegetarianism. The sleep place is simple.

In this view of the turtle's abandonment of the apparent wrath of society also contributes to the practice of destruction as the story of the turtle avoiding accident that lives on its own as in the following Buddha passage:

"Like a tortoise, so is he who is clothed, unreliable to anyone, perfectly destroyed, in his tortoise he gathers all hearts,
Do not hurt anyone, do not speak badly to anyone."

VI. THE METAPHYSICAL WORLD IS THE MAIN PART OF THE CREATION.
At the BB/Original Mind is animated by the False thought, EM changes its status by generating the Dark Force and DM (with its elementary particles that are invisible because of beyond Quantum level), creating the Universe consisting of MW. After creating beyond Quantum particles, more prominent and visible Quantum particles consisting of Neutrino, photos, and other larger elementary particles are generated. These particles form the PW. Likely, PW was created for the primary purpose of teaching sinners. Photons and larger elementary particles prevent beings

from the PW from recognizing or entering the MW, a fact similar to the event in which Adam, Eve, and his offspring were guarded from re-entering Eden Garden, as the Bible writes.

> *Genesis 3:23-4:16*
> New International Version
> [23] So the LORD God banished him from the Garden of Eden to work the ground from which he had been taken. [24] After he drove the man out, he placed on the east side[a] of the Garden of Eden cherubim and a flaming sword flashing back and forth to guard the way to the tree of life.

So, humans know nothing about SH, but the SH world knows all things about the world, as expressed by the saying in the people: "People make, Heaven look."

VII. THE MEANING OF THE LORD'S REDEMPTION OF MANKIND IN THE PHYSICAL WORLD

Jesus Christ or Buddha is the embodiment or the manifestation of the Holy Spirit or Buddhood. The Holy Spirit or Buddhood is the manifestation of the EM, the source of the Creation of the Universe. His power is infinite. The salvation of suffering, illness, and catastrophes may be seen as a small job, but God does not do so because GOD needs to teach people rather than spoil or indulge. Reeducation, according to Christianity or Buddhism, is the core.

> *Luke 9:57-62* [57] As they were walking along the road, a man said to him, "I will follow you wherever you go." [58] Jesus replied, "Foxes have dens and birds have nests, but the Son of Man has no place to lay his head." [59] He said to another man, "Follow me." But he replied, "Lord, first let me go and bury my father."
> [60] Jesus said to him, "Let the dead bury their own dead, but you go and proclaim the kingdom of God." [61] Still another said, "I will follow you, Lord; but first let me go back and say goodbye to my family." [62] Jesus replied, "No one who puts a hand to the plow and looks back is fit for service in the kingdom of God."
>
> *Matthew 5:17-19*
> [17] Think not that I am come to destroy the law, or the prophets: I am not come to destroy, but to fulfil. [18] For verily I say unto you, Till Heaven and earth pass, one jot or one tittle shall in no wise pass from the law, till all be fulfilled. [19] Whosoever therefore shall break one of these least commandments, and shall teach men so, he shall be called the least in the kingdom of Heaven: but whosoever shall do and teach them, the same shall be called great in the kingdom of Heaven.

New Testament often writes about the salvation performed by Jesus through the fact that He came down into this world to cleanse sins and to redeem the sins of believers, such as:

Jesus descends from above" (Is 63,19) begins
Jesus began His ministry by being baptized in the Jordan River, when "the Heavens opened up" (Matt 3,16; Mark 1,9; Luke 3,21) God reveals His Son to mankind. (Mark 1,11; 9,7; 15,38-39). For human himself cannot go up to Heaven to contemplate the "mystery hidden in God." (Ephesians 3,9; John 1,18; 3,13; Rome 10,6), So God sent His Son to bring the revelation to the earth: "My father gave me everything. And no one knows the Son except the Father, and no one knows the Father except the Son and whom the Son will reveal to." (Matt 11,27; John 1,19; 3,11; 14,

1John 2:2
He is the atoning sacrifice for our sins, and not only for ours but also for the sins of the whole world.

John 1:29
[29] The next day John saw Jesus coming toward him and said, "Look, the Lamb of God, who takes away the sin of the world!

1 John 4:10 — The New International Version (NIV)
[10] This is love: not that we loved God, but that he loved us and sent his Son as an atoning sacrifice for our sins.

Revelation 1:6: To him who loves us and has freed us from our sins by his blood, [6] and has made us to be a kingdom and priests to serve his God and Father—to him be glory and power for ever and ever

Romans 5:19 in the English Standard Version (ESV) of the Bible says, "For as by the one man's disobedience the many were made sinners, so by the one man's obedience the many will be made righteous"

2Corin 5:15[15] *he died for all, that those who live should no longer live for themselves but for him who* died for them and was raised again

Matthew 20:28
just as the Son of **Man did not come to be served, but to serve, and to give his life** as a ransom for many."

Mark 10:45
[45] For even the Son of Man did not come to be served, but to serve, and to give his life as a ransom for many."

Corinthians 15:3, "For what I received I passed on to you as of first importance: that Christ died for our sins according to the Scriptures"

The difference between God and Buddha is that the Bible writes many times that God performs miracles that heal the blind, immediate appearance before the disciple, resurrection of the dead... But in the same way, Buddha used miracles to help disciples like Mr. A Nan see the boundaries of SH, listen to the lecture of Buddha... Purpose is to be a means of educating beings, not of eliminating the hindrances in the world.

After the Buddha left the world, people who have faith or belief in Buddhism to keep the rules or laws and practice, meditate and follow the path of liberation. This proves that the Buddha's salvation makes them save themselves.

The ultimate fact cannot be denied so that the Buddha has directly removed all or part of the sin or Karma of those who have sought to follow the Buddha. Of Buddhism, thanks to the effectiveness of 500 years of the perfecr era of Buddhism many people have attained the level Arahat, or the time of Jesus many people have achieved the Sainthood position, not to mention the 12 apostles who follow Him.

Nowadays, the degenerative era of Buddhism and Christianity witnessing a decline in faith due to the fact that the Church attendance every Sunday decreased significantly, maybe the grace of the Buddha or Jesus has also decreased a lot unless the person who has faith and determination to cultivate himself repented. Miracles happen only so that humán know that miracles are only a means for the consolidation of the followers belief.

Therefore it is possible to say that removal of suffering causes (sickness, natural disaster) in this world did not occur either at the presence or after the Buddha /Jesusleft this world. In other words, as it means in the Catechism of the Catholic Church. this PW is perfect for humans to **study, cultivate and repair the mistakes and not to live for fun.**

Humans come into this world just like students who go to school and recruit in military schools, enduring hardship. The misery human beings encounter in life is created by God as a teaching tool. People commit sins in many lives. The sin is the Karma. The idea that praying in the event of an accident, the Buddha will save each one of us in the PW is a great mistake. Miracles occur only so that the living beings know that the Lord is in PW, that Heaven is the homeland, and that Heaven is not to save each person. It is necessary to repent to cleanse the sin and Karmas to be liberated, as in an example in the following sutra

> *As presented in the Lotus Sutra, the parable tells the story of a wealthy man with many children who are playing inside of his house. The house catches on fire, but the children are distracted by their games and they are unaware that the house is burning. In fact, they do not understand what fire is or even what a house is. Thus, in order to lure his children from the house, the wealthy man promises his children that he has three different types of carts waiting for them outside of the house for them to play in: a goat-cart, a deer-cart, and a bullock-cart. When the children rush out of the house to play with their new carts, the three different carts promised by their father are not there. Instead, their father presents them with a single jeweled carriage drawn by a pure white ox.*

In this parable, the three promised carts were skillful means to lure the children out of the house.

In the above example chapter, some people have fun in life without worrying about learning. Therefore, it is necessary only to show people that the MW landscape is more beautiful than this world that begets a worry about learning and that cleanses itself of sin, escapes itself from suffering, and returns home to the place where there is everlasting happiness.

Therefore it is possible to say that abandoning suffering (sickness, natural disaster) in this world did not occur either at Buddha time of presence or after Buddha left this world. In other words, as it means in the BIBLE OF THE CHURCH OF JUSTICE, this built world is perfect for human beings of the earth to study and not to live for fun.

VIII. THE MEANING OF LAW AND THE REDEMPTION
The world is a prison, a school of reformation for sinners from the Metaphysical realm. So the law and punishment apply to sinful people, but do more sins and disturb the learning environment in the PW. The law of the PW is built on the tangible foundation of CS; there is no notion of MW or Karma, so there are shortcomings and many errors. The Karmas from previous lives largely cause the action of each individual; this event is only known in the world of MW and not understandable in the PW. So, the laws of the PW have only relative meaning and can be reasonable for mild and limited punishments in time. The punishment with the death penalty is usually beyond the worldly authority.

THE TWELVE LINKS OF DEPENDENT ORIGINATION

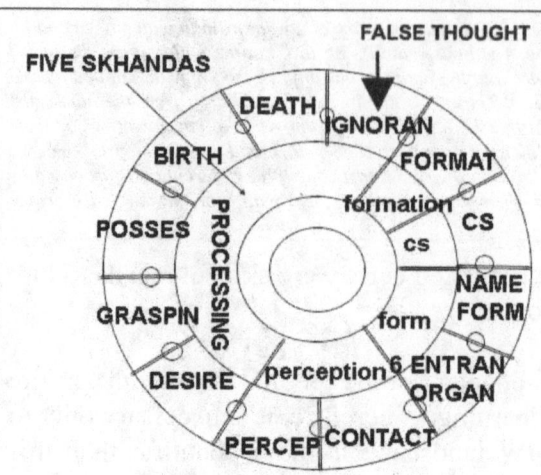

EM is initially activated by a Thought. Suppose it is a False thought in the case of reincarnation. In that case, Ignorance is created, manifested as Form, physical body, and brain. In the beasts, invisibility is expressed through the shape and brain.

2. Formation: Mechanism of transformation of data into CS. In reincarnation is the enSoulment into the next life's physical body. Many Buddhist philosophers have created a new terminology for reincarnation Karma to distinguish it from common Karma. Maybe reincarnation Karma is a selection from the pool of Karma to be active in the next life. The Karmic reminder is the store Karma that is not very active in the next life. In addition to reincarnation Karma, other contributing factors in rebirth are the will, preference, and wishes of the parents. As a result, reincarnation is a selective and critical process in multiple matching. Buddha pointed out that rebirth is as difficult as the story of a blind turtle encountering a log in the vast sea.

3. CS: Following the Formation, the enSoulment eventually transcribes the reincarnation Karma (memories of previous lives) to the brain in the DMN. The insertion of MM corresponds to the formation of 52 inner Minds, called Cetasleka.

4. Name and Form: The inner CS is initially formed with Cetaleska along with five sensory organs.

5. Six senses: Mechanism of receiving data and corresponding CS

6. contact with the outside world. 7. Perception: receiving information.

8-12: The process of feeling makes instant reflex reactional to information, and the process of integrating information makes memory/communication/TR

After Creation, the Twelve-link Circle moves clockwise without beginning or ending. Dependent origination (Paṭiccasamuppāda) is distinct from Conditional Relations (Paṭṭhāna). Conditional Causation sums up all the causes, such as rice needs seeds, weather, and labor, while dependent origination refers to the main cause generating the result, such as the rice plant needs the grain for germination.

The Twelve link circle is the law of Creation; the beginning of Creation is the original root of Ignorance. The 12-link circle can be shortened as five components represented by the five Skandha since the latter also represents the process of the Creation of the Universe.

Breaking the circle for the termination of the birth-death circle can be performed at any link. Although the link between Love and Attachment may be often suggested, the Linh Igngroace is the most critical. It is difficult to get rid of the Love-Attachment link because they are related to Greed, Anger, and Ignorance Minds. On the other hand, breaking the Ignorance link appears to be a more radical approach to solving the problem of reincarnation.

In neuroscience, the desired conduct originates from the Insula, the nucleus of the Amygdala, and Nac, which usually inhibit the brain's moralistic cortex in the Prefrontal cortex.

CONCLUSIONS
People often ask who I am, why I am in this sphere of existence, and what to do.
The CS cannot answer questions of such an existential nature, that is, by philosophy or science, because CS limits the magnitude and complexity of all events and things by the brain and the senses.

In Christianity or Buddhism, the spiritual scriptures indicate that the human is the child of the Holy Spirit or Buddhood/GOD, who should have eternal life and complete happiness. They mistakenly think that all things in the world are good, but in reality, they can be good or bad. Confusion of Bad for Good is a critical mistake; in Christianity, it is equivalent to eating forbidden fruit in Eden Garden. In Buddhism, it is the False thought. Mistakes need to be learned to correct. The Earthly World is the realm created by God and Nirvana. The PW is a school with many challenging lessons to cultivate, but sometimes the Mind is also aroused to recognize pleasures or happiness as in Heaven in a short time.

As a child of the Lord, man should enjoy eternal life and happiness. Those in the Earthly world are the Lord's children but make mistakes accumulated from many lives, so they have been deprived of Original Mind, Omniscience, and many other noble functions. Those in the PW are sent from Heaven down, coated by coarse structure, equipped with the brain primarily to learn and overcome every suffering challenge as recruits in military schools for training or students sent into internship in strictly disciplined schools. Evidence shows that human beings are born to experience suffering before they enjoy the pleasure and live in harsh environments. To survive suffering is to follow the Path of Perfection and eliminate evil Minds. When one graduates, one becomes moral and returns to the homeland.

The problem is simple, but people in the Earthly world are often lofty, do not realize that they have many mistakes or sin, lack morality, and deny the need for reformation, so always striving to seek eternal salvation is sunk in the cycle of reincarnation.

1. WHO IS THE CREATOR/GOD?.

Emptiness/EM created the Universe and creatures. EM is the primordial beginning of Creation since it is EM, it has no precedence, no time, and no space. EM is the only one with itself, homogeneity, and hypersymmetry, which have the potential to be omnipotent and omniscient. After a thought or a start motion, EM undergoes a transformation to have space-time, omnipotence, and Omniscience. Thus, it can be said that, from a conception of Creation, the Creator, manifested as the omnipotent and omniscient, stepped out of EM to create the Universe and creatures. This beginning time is inconceivable. Creation is inherent to the principle of successive Birth and Death, so the Universe will be eventually destroyed according to this principle of successive Birth and Death, such as Sir Penrose's Conformal Cyclic Cosmology/CCC. So Buddha often called it an unimaginable beginning.

The beginning is the manifestation of the so-called Ultimate Force/Dark Force and the Omnscience/Dark Force.

2. THE CREATION INITIATED BY FALSE THOUGHT

- Ultimate Omniscience, which is activated by the right thought, generates ingeniosity and limited awareness.
- Omnipotence generates.

 - The unlimited energy accounts for the Universe's expansion (Dark Force or Ultimate Force).

 - Beyond Quanrum elementary particles and the magnificent and ingenious structures built on the beyond Quantum elementary particles, which the human five senses cannot see,

The combination of Almighty power and UO is the manifestation of the Almighty God that humans can imagine, and above all imagination that is often called a miracle, only existing in Heaven and nirvana.

3. THE CREATION INITIATED BY FALSE THOUGHT

EM is a Creator who never makes mistakes; therefore, there is always the Right Thought. However, in the following step of the Creation, there may be False thought, this error originating from a mistake.

a) REALM OF GRAVITY AND DARK MATTER.
- Consciousness: Because of False thought, UO is remarkably limited in extent and depth., so in the Creation, due to the sense of force is weaker than raw material meditation, and narrowed knowledge becomes Unwise and stupid.
- Energy and Forces are limited in strength and characterized by.
- gravity, combined with
- Dark Matter. Elementary particles and structure are coarser than in Heaven; Creature or sentient in this realm cannot get access to the Haven

There is no Buddha or Heavenly light in this realm, so the darkness obliterates the realm. Part of this realm is Hell. Gravity and DM manifest the sin or Karma caused by mistakes.

b) PHYSICAL WORLD/REALM.
- Consciousness: Because of False thought, UO is remarkably limited in extent and depth., so in the Creation, due to the sense of force, it is weaker than raw material meditation, and narrowed knowledge becomes Unwise and stupid.
- Energy and Forces are limited in strength and characterized by.
- gravity, combined with
- Dark Matter. Elementary particles and structure are coarser than in Heaven; Creature or sentient in this realm cannot get access to the Haven

There is no Buddha or Heavenly light in this realm, so the darkness obliterates the realm. Part of this realm is Hell. Gravity and DM manifest the sin caused by mistakes or Karma. So it can be said that the HH world is the grace of the HST to help those who make mistakes have a chance to return to Heaven. This opportunity is as rare and precious as case of a blind turtle in the open sea encountering a wooden hole floating indefinitely. This opportunity should not be wasted because of a temporary passion for material pleasure.

In the superior levels of the Passion realm, there are no beings like the PW, but there are Souls that manifest Karma and DM. This is intermediate between the PW and Nirvana

c) NON-DUALISTIC SPIRITUAL PATH

Nirvana, or the Highest level of Heaven, represents the Primordial Duality Realm. The Ultimate Realm or EM is absolute and cannot be imagined or expressed in words; on the contrary, the Duality Realm is impermanent and illusion but easily expressed in words and imagined. So, as pointed out by Bodhisatva Nagarjuna

in The Middle Way, the concept of the Middle Way is not attached to existence (EM), and to Non-Existence (Illusion) and is appropriate for attaining the Enlightenment. Buddha, Bodhisatva, and Arahat, the three levels of Nirvana, represent the space-time of Nirvana, in which the Master exists in the Oneness realm but can manifest in the Duality Realm. For example, Bodhisatsava performs the Salvation in the Duality Realm with egolessness. As a result, there is no concept of the giver and the recipient in the act of donation. All Happiness and Affliction need to be conceived like this: do not cling to Affliction or Happiness because Affliction is Bodhi (Salvation), and Happiness is momentary in this worldly Realm. Similarly, in Meditation, Stillness is critical in obtaining fruitful contemplation, but contemplation of Realm of Loving Kindness/Happiness will eventually disturb the stillness. Stillness without contemplation eventually leads to an inert block of wood or stone of Neither Thinking Nor Non-Thinking. Omniscience, the end result of contemplation, is independent of Stillness or Contemplation. That is the non-Dualistic road approaching to Enlightenment realization.

NOBLE EIGHTFOLD PATH

Understanding that the purpose of life is necessary for the practice of Right Mindfulness and the concept of right livelihood (Egolessness). Mindfulness and egolessness are critical in the distinction between the right or deviated expression through thinking, spoken words, and choosing the profession and duty in working places. The purpose of life in the earthly world is to be responsible toward oneself and to help others cultivate morality. So, improving life, environmental conditions, and entertainment have only supportive roles. Building luxurious facilities in living environments for entertainment is likely not appropriate. Momentary pleasure and recreation are not aimed at distracting the main purpose of life, which is spiritual learning for moral perfection. Duty and mission are only to serve the public welfare, to help people in the nation, society, and community to raise morality and spiritual values, and to facilitate spiritual learning. Contrarily, pursuing materialistic personal interests with invasive or offensive acts to neighbors, lands, or countries decreases morality and creates serious karma.

Therefore, in this world, wealth, education, knowledge status, and high social authority are the advantages if serving the public moral interests but can be a great obstacle to the path of spiritual perfection.

d) SCIENCE AND LIFE

The world is a school for learning, not for fun and enjoyment. So, things that go too far from enjoying reasonable pleasure can be considered an erring into sin. Advances in science, in space exploration, ocean exploration, and environmental research, if for the purpose of improving convenience for life and health, are acceptable. Also, art and music have educational value; however, distraction from learning is not a small sin. Evidence of numerous kingdoms collapsed when the kings or royal court officials were deeply involved in distraction and entertainment. Travel stimulates economic development and health care, but too much entertainment is wasteful. More importantly, science disrupts, increases the entropy of the world, destroys nature for urban construction, pollutes the environment, and develops murder weapons, abortion, and transgender medical techniques. Science is the most important factor in degrading moral beliefs. No matter how advanced the science is, the result is too small and incomparable with the MW and Paradise.

But science also improves life in the healing health service that benefits life in spiritual learning and practice. So, scientific development needs to be oriented toward spiritual practice with reasonable pleasure.

e) MERIT IN THE SPIRITUAL PRACTICE.

The purpose of life in this world is to learn spiritual practice. Activities other than learning have a supporting role in learning. The art, entertainment, construction of physical structures, and scientific search for curiosity are of very little merit and may be a fault. Buddhist sutras write that reading one passage in a sutra is more worthy than giving thousands of jewelry. This demonstrates that understanding Buddhist Dharmas is immensely valuable in the practice of giving. *Emperor Wu of Liang* is often compared to King Ashoka (Former Emperor of the Maurya Empire) Buddhist revival in India, and has adopted the Full commandments for Sangha (for Arahat /Theravada) but is considered still having no merit by the Bodhidharma. It may be that the sacrifice to the King is too easy. Buddhism at the time was not well developed despite a significant number of followers and the lack of sutras and books. Therefore, Buddhist Dharma is one of the three jewels of Buddhism.